AF538955

BUSINESS AND SOCIETY

Business and Society

Dr. P.G. Aquinas

ANMOL PUBLICATIONS PVT. LTD.
NEW DELHI - 110 002 (INDIA)

ANMOL PUBLICATIONS PVT. LTD.
H.O.: 4374/4B, Ansari Road, Darya Ganj,
New Delhi-110 002 (India)
Ph.: 23278000, 23261597
B.O.: No. 1015, Ist Main Road, BSK IIIrd Stage
IIIrd Phase, IIIrd Block,
Bangalore - 560 085 (India)
Visit us at: www.anmolpublications.com

Business and Society

PRINTED IN INDIA

Printed at Mehra Offset Press, Delhi.

To

My wife

Theresa L. Aquinas

For her unconditional love,
Intellectual enlightenment and
Support

My Cherished Daughters

Lishel & Leann

For being the kind of daughters
fathers dream about

CONTENTS

PREFACE

This book has been written with a view to present a simple text for BBM Degree students of Mangalore University and other Universities where students are pursuing "Business and Society" as a subject of their curricula.

The book purports to be an introduction to the subject "Business and Society". Being a text book, I do not claim any originality about the subject-matter. I have drawn upon the available scattered material and tried to assimilate it with a view to presenting it in a clear and readable language.

The treatment of the subject is lucid and its coverage comprehensive. The main intention is to capture the essence of the subject without burdening the student with long and elaborate theoretical explanations. At the end of each chapter, review questions have been given for recapitulation and better grasp of the subject. University questions are also given at the end of the chapter keeping in view the requirement of the students who will take up the University examination. A separate chapter on "case studies" has been included to present current issues in real-life settings that allow for critical analysis.

As the book has been written keeping in view the course content of "Business and Society" of Mangalore University, question papers of the aforesaid examination have been included at the end of the book.

Any suggestion for the improvement of the book would be welcome and gratefully acknowledged and made use of in the subsequent edition.

06th May 2005 **P.G. AQUINAS**

ACKNOWLEDGEMENTS

One of the most pleasant parts of writing this textbook is the opportunity to thank those who have contributed to it in several ways. Many people played important roles in the development of this book, I am deeply grateful to them. Ultimately any errors of omission or commission are mine, and I bear responsibility for them.

Several people at Anmol Publications Pvt., Ltd. were especially helpful, Mr. J.L. Kumar, Managing Director, Mr. Kripal D. Joshi, Production Manager and the production team members. It has been a pleasure to work with each of these individuals.

The excellent sales team at Anmol made this venture a memorable one Mr. V. Srinavasa Murthy – Regional Sales Executive (South) and his team of dedicated sales executives were very supportive and have envisioned great interest in the publication of this book. I whole heartily thank them for their precious support.

I sincerely acknowledge the moral support and inspiration by Mr. S. S Rao of Sita Book House Mangalore.

My special thanks are due to Mrs Shamala Shetty, Mrs Jyothi Shetty, Ms. Hemavathi and Ms. Pallavi, Faculty of Computer Science, and Ms. Sowmya Rao, Lecturer MBA Department, NMAM Institute of Technology, Nitte.

I wish to place on record the help extended by my colleagues in the MBA Department, St. Aloysius College, Dr.

Prakesh Pinto Sr. Lecturer, and Mrs. Diana Saldhana Lecturer. Mr. Praveen D'Souza Librarian. I also thank Mr Santhosh Pinto, Lecturer, Commerce Department St. Aloysius College for his valuable suggestions.

Finally, I thank my family - my wife Mrs. Theresa L. Aquinas and my Daughters Lishel and Leann - for the unselfish love, endless patience, and quite understanding that allowed me to devote such a large part of my life to my career. Truly, without their willingness to assume many of the tasks necessary to produce a text book and their scarifies that allowed me the time needed to prepare it, this book would never have been completed. Their continued patience, support and interest in the progress of my work made writing this book a pleasant task.

06th May 2005

P. G. AQUINAS

1

BUSINESS OBJECTIVES AND ENVIRONMENT

Learning Objectives

After going through this chapter, you will be conversant with:

- Business and its environment
- Business Objectives
    1. Organic objectives
    2. Economic objectives
    3. Social objectives
    4. Human objectives
    5. National objectives

The term "business" refers to commercial activities aimed at making a profit. Economic theory makes a fundamental assumption that profit maximization is the basic objective of every firm. This old concept of business, confining it to commerce and industry meant specifically for private profit has undergone a radical change. The modern outlook is different. For many organizations, profit maximization in the short run is not the primary objective. For them, profit is only secondary. Today, business is regarded as a social institution forming an integral part of the social system. According to Davis and Blomstorm—"A business is a social institution, performing a social mission and having a broad influence on the way people live and work together". According to this definition, business refers to the development and processing of economic values in society. It performs a social mission and is viewed as a sub-system of the total social system.

Business is thus an integral part of the society. It influences other elements of society, which in turn, affect business. The type of products to be manufactured, marketing strategies to be adopted etc., are influenced by the society. The society on the other hand is influenced by the way business functions. The organization of the business, innovations, new ideas etc., may affect society. Business activities have greatly influenced social attitudes, values, outlooks, customs, traits etc. However, it is difficult to change many elements of the social environment at least, in the short run. Hence, Business has to adapt to the society. In order to succeed, a business must have values, viability and public visibility.

1. *Value:* Business must develop certain values for which they stand. Values are a source of institutional drive. These values become guides for employees besides becoming strong motivators for the employees.

2. *Visibility:* Visibility means the drive to live, grow and achieve. If a business is to be a visible organization, it must initiate its share of forces in its own environment. It must become a trend setter rather than a meek follower.

3. *Public Visibility:* Public visibility refers to the extent to which its acts are known. A business is an integral part of the social system. Its activities are therefore to be subjected to public judgment. Therefore, public visibility becomes important for a business.

BUSINESS AND ITS ENVIRONMENT

The environment factors have a profound impact on business. Business is in fact dependent on the environment. The environment in which an individual or an organization operates has a more or less direct bearing on its objectives and functions. This applies to a business organization as well as to any other type of organization. A proper estimate of the objectives of business can therefore be made only after an understanding of the environment in which a business firm functions. The environment in which an individual or an organization operates has a more or less direct bearing on its objectives and functions. This applies to a business organization as well as it does to any other type of organization. A proper estimate of the objectives of a business can therefore be made only after an understanding of the environment in which a business firm functions. It must be noted here that the environmental factors are beyond the control of a firm and therefore, its success will depend to a very large extent on its adaptability to the environment. The environment of a business enterprise comprises of several segments which may be classified as under:-

Social: Comprising customers and employees as well as social institutions which benefit from business or provide benefits to it;

Economic: Encompassing the whole economy, the various economic institutions including the other firms with which a firm has to deal;

Political: Covering the political institutions of the country including the government and the legislature which regulate business activity and draw upon the resources of the business firm in the form of taxes of different kinds and

Technology: Comprising the know-how and production and management technology available to business firms at any point or period of time.

The relationship between a firm and its environment is one of mutual benefit. The environment of a firm will be to take stock of the various interest groups which are contributors to the firm's continuity and prosperity and also claimants of returns in different forms from the business firms. These groups include consumers, employees, stock-holders, creditors, suppliers, distributors, competitors and the government. The survival and growth of a business firm will depend upon its relations with all these interest groups. The diagram below shows the firm in relations to the different interest groups that constitute its environment.

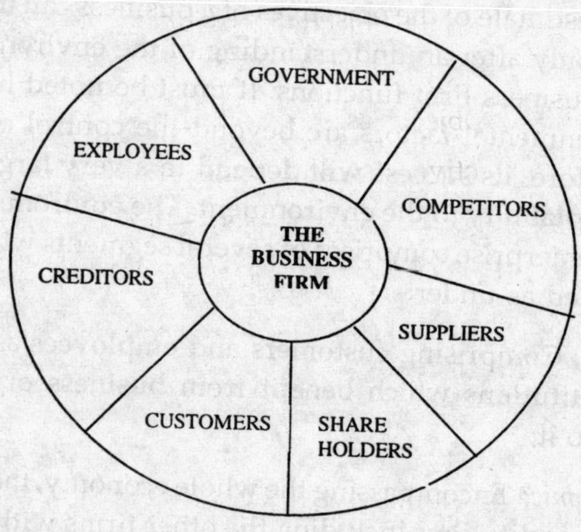

Fig 1.1: The Business firm and its environment.

BUSINESS OBJECTIVES

The objective with which a business concern is established and run depends upon many factors. They depend largely on the socio-economic-political set up of the country. In capitalist countries like U.S.A, profit maximization is the main objective. Whereas, in socialist countries, the main objective of business has been maximum output rather than profit. But in mixed economy, profit is not allowed to be the chief objective and every business organization is required to set its objectives keeping in view the socio-economic-political structure of the society in which it operates.

The concept of objectives is fundamental to a business enterprise. Objectives explain why a business was set up and helps to guide the activities and behaviour of businessmen. It is significant to note that it is very difficult to outline precisely the single objective of a business. A business has multiple objectives. We may broadly classify the various objectives of business as follows:-

1. Organic Objectives.
2. Economic Objectives.
3. Social Objectives.
4. Human Objectives.
5. National Objectives.

The first two objectives i.e., Organic Objectives and Economic Objectives help the business directly. The other three Objectives i.e., Social Objectives, Human Objectives and National Objectives help the business indirectly.

1. Organic Objectives

A business enterprise is essentially an organic entity. As an organic entity, a business enterprise has its own stages of infancy, childhood, adolescence, adulthood and maturity. Like a human being, an enterprise first works towards the objective of survival. When the enterprise is assured of its survival, it looks forward to growth and expansion with goodwill, prestige and recognition. Organic objectives are the foundation for achieving all other objectives of a business. Thus, survival, growth and prestige appear to be the typical objectives of the business firm. The organic objectives of a business firm are -

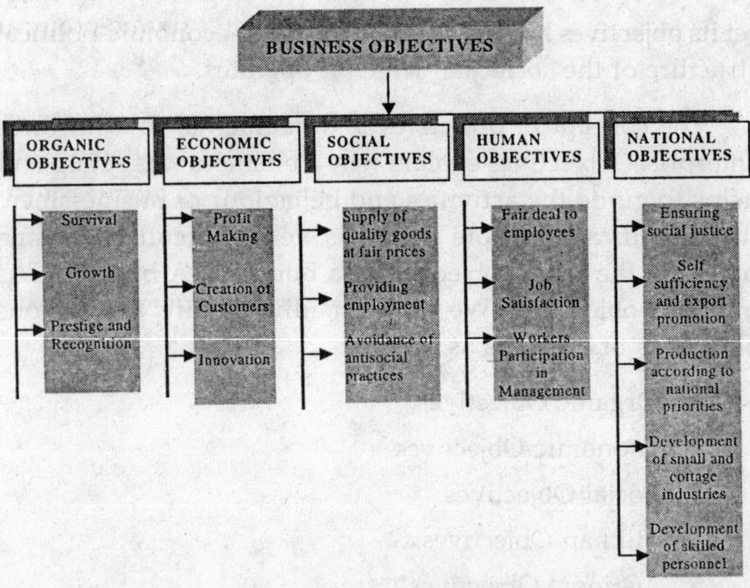

Fig. 1.2: Business objectives

(a) *Survival:* First of all a business enterprise tries to maintain its existence. Among objectives related to survival, we may include the maintenance of firm's competitive position, the earning of sufficient income, protecting itself against adverse legislation and market standing. Unless an enterprise survives no other objective can be accomplished.

(b) *Growth:* Growth is one of the major objectives of business. Growth is measured in terms of size, investment, market share etc. Growth brings higher profits, economic and social power etc. Thus, for some firms growth may be more important than profit-maximization.

(c) *Prestige and Recognition:* The development of a prestige position for a firm may assure survival and aid growth. A business enterprise with good image and goodwill can easily attract customers, investors and competent employees. Prestige and recognition however may be pursued directly as well.

2. Economic Objectives

A Business firm is an economic entity and therefore, its main objectives are economic. The economic objectives of business are as follows: -

a) Profit Making.

b) Creation of Customer.

c) Innovation.

(a) Profit making: For quite a long time, it was held that the sole objective of business was maximization of profit. But this is no longer a universally valid business objective. According to Urwick, "Earning of profits cannot be the objective of a business any more than eating is the objective of living". A business unit is as economic entity in which various factors of production are used.

Capital is one of the factors of production and the reward for investing capital is given in the form of profit. Therefore, a business should not be run to maximize the reward of one factor of production only through it is true that existence of profit is necessary to induce the people to invest money in business ventures.

Today, profit is not the primary objective of a business. A business may strive to maintain or gain leadership in market share, sales volume, fixed assets, employment etc., and even sacrificing profit maximization. However, a reasonable level of profit is necessary for the successful running of a business. As Goyder states —"in the responsible company, profits will continue to be the creation of financial health as blood is the life of man, so are profits the life of industry, and just as man must maintain life before he can be free to pursue the life's objectives, he has set before him, so profits are necessary to business and are in the proper sense of the word 'primary'. But profits are not the ultimate objects of responsible company".

It has been emphasized that the objectives of a business enterprises are shaped in a large measure by its obligations to the various parts of its environment. Since the environment of a business firm comprises several interest groups, it must have a multiplicity of objectives, instead of a single objective, profit, which has been traditionally over-emphasized. There are five areas in which objectives of performance and results have to be set: market standing, productivity, physical and financial resources, profitability, manager performance and development, worker performance and attitude.

(i) *Market Standing:* The profitability creation of a market must always be the objective of a business. Customer is the foundation of all business and business is for most part creation of a customer. For this the business enterprise has to strive persistently to discover the needs of the people and satisfy them through supply of the right goods and service. Markets do not happen by chance. They are the result of the business action which anticipates a need. To establish its standing in the market, the businessman has to be constantly on the search for its customer and has to find out who he is, what he wants, how much he can pay and what else is available to him.

(ii) *Productivity:* Another important objective of a business is productivity. In its attempt to secure perpetual existence and prosperity, a business firm can succeed only if it is conscious of the need to make the best use of the available resources and secure the maximum return with the minimum of input. This calls for the existence of a will to do better on the part of the management and the operative personnel.

(iii) *Physical and Financial Resources:* Yet another important objective of a business is to secure adequate physical and financial resources to be able to supply the goods and services and value satisfaction desired by the customers. The management has the responsibility for planning and acquiring the physical facilities and other resources needed to turn the wheel of production. The maintenance of sufficient assets and resources is, of course, a part of this objectivity.

(iv) *Profitability:* Profitability is yet another objective that a business firm strives to attain. Profit in relation to capital investment is not only a good measure of the net effectiveness and soundness of a business effort but it also serves the purpose of covering costs like replacement, obsolescence, market risk and uncertainty and is necessary to ensure the supply of capital for innovation and expansion. A business must have enough profit to yield the market rate of return on existing investment and to produce the additional capital needed.

(v) *Human resource development:* A business enterprise has also to make conscious attempts for the development of its human resources by keeping a vigilant eye on its manager's and worker's performance and their development. This is important because the human factor is the factor that can be used to activate the other resources and as such it holds the key to the performance of the enterprise in other areas. Thus business can accomplish its economic objectives of innovation and productivity only when the employees are given adequate opportunities for developing new skills and capabilities. Business should create a proper climate wherein the talents of workers are allowed to grow and mature.

(b) Creation of Customer: Business can earn profits only when it provides goods or services which people (customers) are willing to buy. Without customers business makes no-sense. Peter F. Drucker in his book *"The Practice of Management"* says "there is only one valid definition of business purpose; to create a customer. It is the customer who determines what a business is...... The customer is the foundation of business and keeps it in existence....... and it is to supply the customer that society entrusts wealth-producing resources to a business enterprises". From the above quotation, we can say that the objective of business enterprise is to identify what people (customers) want, where they want and when they want and provide them the desired goods and services at the time and place they so desire. A business enterprise cannot survive unless there are enough customers to buy the products and services offered by it. Customer is the generator of revenue for a business firm.

(c) Innovation: The business world today is a competitive world. Business can flourish only if the economy is dynamic and is ever on the move. This can happen only if every branch of business is on the alert and true to discover ways and means of improving, changing, and enriching the entire operation. Innovation may be of two kinds:

(i) Innovation in product or service, and

(ii) Innovation in the various skills and techniques needed to supply them.

A business enterprise that stops innovating slows down, stagnates and is left behind in the race of competition. A successful firm has not only to adjust itself to changing environment; it must on its own create conditions favourable to survival and growth. The highly competitive nature of modern business puts a premium on innovation and creativity which implies the introduction of new and better products, improved means of production, new technology, new methods and procedures of management, etc., otherwise a business firm may not be able to continue for long.

3. Social Objectives

All institutions including business are tool of society. Therefore, the economic objectives of business can be realized only by serving the society. Organizations are established by society and in the long run they continue to exist with the consent of society. A really successful business can be built on the foundation of social service. If a business serves the various sections of society, profits will automatically follow. In fact, we can say that profits are the reward which a business earns by serving society.

A business organization's social role is not rigid. It evolves gradually in response to the human needs of that society. It may change its way of working with other organization, it may change the activities it performs, it may change its way of working with people etc. Therefore, we may say that as society changes, it inevitably brings about a change in the role of business.

Social objectives of business refer to the obligations of business towards customers, employees, investors, suppliers, Government and the general public. The social objectives of a business especially in an underdeveloped country are expected to be as follows:-

(a) Quality goods at fair prices.

(b) Providing Employment.

(c) Avoiding profiteering and anti-social practices.

(a) Quality Goods at Fair Prices: A business is excepted to supply goods of right quality at a fair price. Today, consumers are conscious of the quality of goods they buy. When goods

are of sub-standard quality or adulterated, they stop buying such goods. This will force a business to close down. Therefore, in the long run, only those business enterprises which meet the basic demand of the society will survive. Thus, every business enterprise must maintain a continuous and adequate supply of articles of standard quality at reasonable and fair prices.

(b) Providing Employment: In an underdeveloped country, providing employment is the most important social objective of a business. A business is required to create opportunities for gainful employment of the people. This objective can be met by undertaking new projects or by expanding the existing ones especially in backward areas. These projects not only provide employment to the residents but also add to the overall prosperity of the area. Further, the Government of India is also extending full co-operation to the business by providing infrastructural facilities etc., this should be made use of by business to their advantage.

However, the objective of providing employment may sometimes conflict with the economic objective of cutting down costs and improving profits by introducing automation. When this situation arises priority should be given to providing employment. This is necessary in a country like India. Therefore mechanization may have to be deferred or implemented gradually in stages without causing loss of jobs to anyone.

(c) Avoidance of Profiteering and Anti-Social Practices: Every society recognizes the claim of business to a reasonable profit. No business can justify exploitation of the consumers through overcharging and creating artificial scarcities. It is an important social responsibility of the business to make the goods and services available to consumers at a reasonable price and not indulge in hoarding, black-marketing, adulteration and other anti-social practices. Moreover, in times of scarcity, it should

ensure fair and equitable distribution of commodities. Every society expects a business enterprise to adopt socially responsible and ethical behaviour and be fair in its dealings with various groups in society.

4. Human Objectives

A business enterprise is an institution carried on by people (owners), through people (employees) for people (consumers and public). Therefore, human factor pervades all business activities. It is therefore necessary for a business to look after the interest of those who make business successful. People are the most valuable asset of business and their well-being is its main concern. In fact, since the Hawthorne experiments conducted by Elton Mayo and his associates, it has been widely recognized that human beings should be treated as individuals. Such an approach contributes to higher productivity through job satisfaction. The success of a business depends upon the quality of people working in it. In order to win the co-operation of employees, business must fulfil their expectation. The human objectives of business arise from these expectations. Thus a business should provide for:

(a) Fair Deal to Employees.

(b) Job-Satisfaction and

(c) Workers Participation in Management.

(a) Fair Deal to Employees: Employee welfare is no less important than customer satisfaction. They should be given fair wages, salaries and incentives. Besides, the work environment should be congenial to human beings and security of services should also be provided. This is necessary for securing the whole-hearted effort of the employees.

(b) Job-Satisfaction: There is an obligation of the business to provide job-satisfaction to its employees. This can be done, by making the job interesting and challenging for the

employees. Selection of right man for the right job and reducing unpleasantness of jobs help in increasing job satisfaction. Further, it should be seen that the job does not become monotonous. A business enterprise is able to fulfil its human objective when it recognizes the dignity of labour.

(c) Workers Participation in Management: Workers participation in management facilitates redressal of employees' grievances quickly and at the lowest possible level. In organizations where employees have been given a representation in management, strikes and lockouts have been replaced by healthy co-operation. Recognition of workers representatives and their legitimate activities help to maintain healthy trade union practices and sound industrial relations. Thus, workers will put forth their best efforts only when they are given an opportunity to participate in making decisions which affect them.

5. National Objectives

National objectives of a business are different from social objectives. They are more specific business obligations towards national needs and aspirations. Present day business is expected to serve as an instrument for the fulfilment of national needs and aspirations and implementation of national plans and policies in accordance with the accepted priorities. In India business organizations have to fulfil the following obligations -

(a) Ensuring Social Justice.
(b) Self-sufficiency and Export Promotion.
(c) Production according to National Priorities.
(d) Development of small scale and cottage industries.
(e) Development of skilled personnel.

(a) Ensuring Social Justice: The overall national objective is to establish growth, stability, and foster social justice. For

this purpose business enterprises should give special attention to the neglected weaker and backward sections and minorities in the society. A business organization can remove inequalities of opportunities and provide a fair opportunity to all work and progress specially the lesser privileged in society.

(b) Self-sufficiency and Export Promotion: - Every business should take adequate steps to boost exports and thereby help the country to earn valuable foreign exchange. Business should also aim at import substitution, so that the country can become self-reliant and self-sufficient.

(c) Production According to National Priorities: - Every business enterprises should manufacture and supply goods necessary for the country's development. Production of essential commodities should be given preference over luxury goods.

(d) Development of Small-Scale and Cottage Industries: - Large business concerns are expected to encourage the growth and development of small and cottage industries. They should patronize the ancillary units by buying their products and providing them financial and technical assistance.

(e) Development of Skilled Personnel: - Business organization can provide training and development to managers and technicians. Skilled managers and technicians are essential for the economic growth of a country. Thus, business can help in the development of skilled personnel.

The various objectives of the business stated above indicate the profound importance of business in modern society. As large amounts of resources are concentrated in the business sector, it should be expected to play a leading role in enhancing the material and social welfare of a nation. Business can significantly assist the development of backward areas, agriculture, export etc., and can make a significant contribution to community development and social welfare. Further they can make a significant contribution of community development and social welfare. Further they can make a significant contribution to research and development and undertake many challenging tasks which can transform the country economically and socially.

QUESTIONS

(For Self Study)

1. "Profit can be no more the objective of business than eating is the object of living" - In light of this statement, explain the motives or objectives of business activities.
2. Enumerate the objectives of modern business.
3. "Business exists to create and deliver value satisfaction at a profit". Critically examine this statement.
4. "Profit is not an objective but a requirement of business". In the light of this statement describe the role of profit-making in business.

UNIVERSITY QUESTIONS

(15 Marks)

- "Profit can be no more the objective of business than eating is the object of living" - In light of this statement, explain the motives or objectives of business activities. (October 2002) (April 1996)
- Explain the inter-relationship of a business organisation and its environment (Oct/Nov – 2004)
- What is Micro-Environment? In what way they affect the performance of a business unit? (Oct/Nov – 2004)
- Explain the role of external environmental factors on the formulation of Business Plans (April – 2004)
- How does a business organisation operate in its environment? What are its inputs and outputs? (April – 2004) (October – 2003)
- "There are basically six changing environmental forces influencing the Business Enterprises" – Assess their importance (April/May – 2003) (October 1996)

- Explain the objectives of Modern Business (April/May – 2003)
- Define Business. What are its important division? (April – 1996)
- Define the term business. What do you consider to be the essential requisites for attaining success in modern business.(October 1996)
- What is meant by Business? Explain its various characteristics.(April/May 1997)
- "Business is a system created to satisfy societies needs and desires" with the background of this statement explain the characteristics of Modern Business (October 2003)

(5 Marks)

- Profitability is the basic economic objective or need of survival of an enterprise – justify (October 1996)

(1 Mark)

- Give any 4 objectives of modern business (April/May 1997)
- Macro Environment (October/November 2004).

2

BUSINESS ETHICS AND SOCIAL VALUE

Learning Objectives

After going through this chapter, you will be conversant with:

- Social Value and Business Ethics
- Types of Business Ethics
- Social Duties and Obligations of Business
  1. Duties of Manufacturers
  2. Duties of Wholesalers
  3. Duties of Retailers
- Social responsibility of Business in India
- Business Ethics in India
  1. Towards Consumers
  2. Towards Employees
  3. Towards Government and Community
- Professionalisation of Management

Business is an integral part of the social system; and it influences other elements of society. The organization of the business, the way the business functions innovations, new ideas etc., may affect society. Business activities have greatly influenced social attitudes, values, outlooks, customs traits etc. Thus, it is true that business influences society. It is also true that society influences business. The type of products to be manufactured and marketed, the marketing strategies to be employed, and the way the business should be organized are all influenced by the society. Hence, a business has to adapt to these uncontrollable external environments.

Business in general refers to the totality of all enterprises in a country, engaged in manufacturing, industry, trade, finance, banking etc. In modern societies, business occupies a dominating place affecting the life of citizens in different ways. Traditionally, the term business commonly referred to commercial activities aimed at making a profit. The economic theory made a fundamental assumption that profit maximization was the basic objective of every firm.

According to Milton Friedman - "The only one social responsibility of business - to use its resources and engage in activities designed to increase its profits". The old concept of business, confining it to commerce and private profit, has undergone a radical change. Today, business is regarded as a social institution forming an integral part of the social system. Therefore, business has to contribute to man's happiness, his freedom and his mental, moral and spiritual growth.

According to Prof. Harold - "In a time when bribes, illegal pay-off, price conspiracies and accusations of irresponsibility. continue to tarnish the image of American business the problem of ethics in the free enterprise system remains a valid and difficult one".

Calkins is of the view that - "It is now recognized that the direction of business is important to the public welfare, that businessmen perform a social function".

David and Blomstorm remarks that business is "a social institution, performing a social mission and having a broad influence on the way people live and work together."

Thus the term business refers to the development and processing of economic values in society. As Rabbi Hillel put it - "If I am not for myself, then who is for me? And if I am not for others then who am I? Thus, the relations between the individual and his actions in the society demands that the need of the individual require that he be for others as well as for himself.

According to Davis and Blomstorm, "Our modern view of society is an ecological one. Ecology is concerned with the mutual relations of human populations or systems with their environment. It is necessary to take this broad view because the influence and involvement of business are extensive. Business cannot isolate itself from the rest of society. Today the whole society is a business's environment".

SOCIAL VALUE AND BUSINESS ETHICS

Social value determines what people consider to be good or bad for society. A business is a part of the society and so it should follow the ethical and moral norms of the society. Business ethics provide a code of conduct for the managers. The purpose of business ethics is to guide the managers in performing their jobs. They should be guided by the principles which are considered right by the society. Ethics are concerned with what is right and what is wrong in human behaviour. They lay down the norms of behaviour by the business. The various parameters of ethical behaviour followed by a business are given below. They are -

1. To charge fair prices from the customers.
2. Make use of correct weights to measure the commodities.
3. To earn reasonable profits for the shareholders.
4. To treat workers in a fair and just manner.
5. To pay taxes to the Government honestly.

1. To Charge Fair Prices from the Customers: Customer's satisfaction is the ultimate aim of all economic activity.

Therefore, the business has its obligations towards the customers. Therefore, it is the duty of the business to

(a) To produce goods which are more satisfying to the consumers and to charge them fair prices for the goods.

(b) To meet the needs of the customers of different classes and different purchasing power.

(c) To make goods of the right quality available at reasonable price.

(d) To distribute the goods and services properly so that the customers do not face any difficulty in purchasing them.

2. *To Make use of Correct Weights to Measure the Commodities*: Adulteration of goods, poor quality, failure to give fair measure, lack of service and courtesy of the customers, misleading or dishonest advertising are some of the examples of violation by business towards its customers. These malpractices should be avoided by the business. The business should:

(a) Provide prompt, courteous service and adequate service to the customers.

(b) To follow fair trade practices and avoid indulging in unfair and unethical practices such as black marketing, hoarding, adulteration etc.

(c) To handle customers grievances with courtesy.

3. *To earn reasonable profit for the shareholders:* The management of a firm is responsible for safeguarding the interests of the shareholders. In the case of sole trader concern and partnership concerns, the owners can look after their own interest as the management of the firm is in its owner's hands. But in the case of a company, the management is in the hands of directors and therefore, the directors have the

following responsibilities towards the shareholders. They are-

(i) The Directors are the trustees of the shareholder's funds. Therefore, the directors must use the assets of the company to increase the welfare of the shareholders.

(ii) Shareholders are a source of funds for the company. They should therefore get reasonable returns for the money invested by them. Therefore, the directors should endeavour to make maximum profits for their company's shareholders.

(iii) The assets of a company are purchased with the funds provided by the shareholders. Therefore, the directors should endeavour to safeguard the assets of the company.

(iv) The directors should see that the company is growing at a steady rate.

(v) The directors should keep the shareholders well informed about the financial position as well as the progress of the company.

To treat Workers in a fair and just manner: The firms should treat workers as human beings. The management should fulfill the following obligations towards the workers.

(i) In order to lead a good life and satisfy their needs every person should earn a reasonable income. Therefore, every business should pay its workers reasonable wages and salaries.

(ii) Besides a fair wage, workers should also be provided with benefits like medical benefits, housing, insurance cover etc.

(iii) Management should give the workers opportunities to develop their capabilities through training, education and the enjoyment of freedom to the greatest possible extent.

(iv) Management should provide the workers with good working conditions.

5. *To Pay Taxes to the Government honestly*: Management should follow fair trade practices. It should pay taxes and other Government dues honestly, fully and promptly. It should not encourage corruption, black marketing and other social evils.

TYPES OF BUSINESS ETHICS

Chester Barnard refers to the following types of moralities in a company. They are -

1. Personal responsibility.
2. Representative or official responsibility.
3. Personal loyalties.
4. Corporate responsibilities.
5. Organizational loyalties.
6. Economic responsibilities.
7. Technical morality.
8. Legal responsibility.

1. *Personal responsibility*: It refers to a man's personal code of ethics. If a man believes in honesty, he will believe in a very honest and straight forward manner. According to Walton, "A morally responsible executive is one who knows the various kinds of value systems that may be employed in a particular situation and has a rather clear idea of what values hold ascendancy (precedence or priority) over others in a conflict". This definition of Walton is rather an over-simplification. A businessman may think he is acting ethically but others may not consider his behaviour as ethical.

2. *Representative or Official Responsibility*: A manager's action often represents the position he holds or the office he occupies rather than his personal beliefs. This is so because the manager represents the business. He has to follow the rules and regulations of the business. For e.g.: a manager may want to do something but the regulations may forbid him from doing it and therefore his hands are tied and he may not do it.

3. *Personal Loyalties:* Sometimes personal loyalties are so strong that ethical standards may not be applied when acting towards a particular individual. Personal loyalties include the loyalties of a subordinate to his superior and superior's loyalty towards his subordinate.

(a) *Loyalties of a subordinate to his superior*: If a subordinate has strong personal loyalty towards their superior, they turn a blind eye towards the blunders committed by their superiors and attempt to defend their omissions and commissions. For e.g.: If the branch manager of a bank is sanctioning loan without any security and this act on his part may bring disastrous financial troubles to the organization, his subordinates who were men of high moral character and who had close connections with the head office may not inform them of the financial irregularities because of strong personal loyalty towards their branch manager.

(b) *Superior's loyalty towards his subordinate*: If a superior has strong personal loyalty towards their subordinates, they turn a blind eye towards the mistakes committed by their subordinates. This is done because the superior does not want to hurt the feeling of his subordinates because of their close personal contact. For e.g.: If the subordinates who are close to the manager do not do their work properly, the manager may not reprimand (rebuke or scold) them for their poor performance. He may rather defend their poor quality work with his superiors because of his personal attachment towards his subordinates.

4. *Corporate Responsibilities*: Every individual living in society has a moral obligation towards it. Corporations are entities which are "artificial persons", therefore they too have moral responsibilities towards the society. There moral responsibilities are not necessarily identical with the personal moral codes of the executives who run them. Every corporation must have moral codes which help it in deciding matters connected with shareholders, employees, creditors, customers, government and society.

5. *Organizational Loyalties:* Some employees have a deep sense of loyalty to the organization. Their loyalties to their organization are so strong that they even neglect their own self interest for the sake of the organization.

6. *Economic Responsibility:* According to Milton Friedman, "there is one and only one social responsibility of business - to use its resources efficiently and engage in activities designed to increase profits without deception or fraud". Therefore, every business must contribute to the general welfare of the society by making efficient and economical use of resource at their command. This type of morality guides individual action towards economy in the use of resources put at his disposal.

7. *Technical Morality:* In any country, the state of technology plays an important role in determining what products and services will be produced. Technological environment influences organizations in terms of investment in technology, consistent application of technology and the effects of technology. A manager having technical morality will refuse to compromise with quality. Every organization which is actively engaged in technological advancement will create more challenging situations for the organizations because they are not prepared to accept lower standards.

8. Legal Responsibility: Legal environment provides the framework within which the business is to function. The viability of business depends upon the ability with which a business can meet the challenges arising out of the legal framework. However, it must be observed here that legal responsibility is more than an intention to conform to laws, orders etc. It is a belief in the need for effective co-operation and justice in organized life. It is morality that transcends conformity to law.

SOCIAL DUTIES AND OBLIGATIONS OF BUSINESS

Organization is neither self-sufficient nor self-contained. They exchange resources with the outside environment and depend on it for their survival. Therefore, organizations have obligations and duties towards society. They draw inputs from society, transform the inputs into goods and services and these goods and services are supplied to society. Businessmen will be judged by their actions. They will have to take due note of new expectations and moods of society. People want immediate decisions and actions to improve their economic conditions. Therefore every business enterprises whether they are producers, wholesalers or retailers must anticipate social needs and convert these needs into opportunities for better performance and better results. The social duties and obligations of business may be divided into three categories depending upon the kind of trade the business men is in.

1. Social Duties and Obligations of Manufacturers.
2. Social Duties and Obligations of Wholesalers.
3. Social Duties and Obligations of Retailers.

1. Social Duties and Obligations of Manufacturers

- Goods product at lowest possible price. Constant

efforts for improving the cost of production so that the consumer can receive better goods at lower prices.

- Correct measures and weights should be used.
- Absence of adulteration.
- Effective service to the consumer.
- Goods produced should reach the ultimate consumers at fixed prices. These price must be printed on the packet to ensure that unscrupulous middlemen do not take the gullible (trusting or naive) consumer for a ride.
- Ethical and informative packing, advertising and sales promotion.

2. Social Duties and Obligations of Wholesalers

- Wholesalers know the pulse of the market. He should therefore enlighten the manufactures about the specific requirements, acceptance, and satisfaction of the customers.
- Wholesalers should not resort to hoarding, profiteering and black-marketing. They should not manipulate the market and create man-made shortages.
- Wholesalers should have fair dealing with retailers.
- Wholesalers should play a positive and constructive role in the economy so as to justify his existence as middlemen.

3. Social Duties and Obligations of Retailers

- Correct weight and measures should be used.
- Reasonable price should be charged.
- Unadulterated goods should only be sold.
- Should not resort to anti-social activities such as hoarding, profiteering, black-marketing etc.

- Provide effective after sales service.
- Offer exchange facilities if consumer is not satisfied with goods.
- Sale on monthly credit. This will help the salaried customers.
- Customers should be provided with choice. Therefore provision should be made to have a wide range of goods.
- He should communicate consumer choice to the manufacturer.

SOCIAL RESPONSIBILITY OF BUSINESS IN INDIA

Social responsibility of business is not a new concept. Leading businessmen of the world have reaffirmed their belief in this concept. If affects their decision and their actions. Businessmen have recognized that since they are managing an economic unit in the society, they have a responsibility to the society. The Indian business sector presents a mixed picture as far as social responsibility is concerned. On the side of production, growth and efficiency, the Indian industry on the whole has done remarkably well. However, on the distributional side its record has been dismal. The size of black market, volume of black money and corruption has been fairly large. It is gratifying to note that a number of leading companies in India have shown recognition for the social responsibility. They have set up institutions of public services like schools, colleges, hospitals, research institutions etc. Thus, the question of social responsibility of business has been gaining the attention of the business community. The Calcutta seminar on the social responsibility of business was held in March 1966. The seminar discussed the main features of social responsibility of business and expressed the need for a special expert study of this problem. Consequently, a special study group was set up. The study group went into the problem and suggested the following guidelines to business. The same is reproduced here below:

1. Business must accept responsibility to the society and its various constituents as a trustee for the goods and services that it produces, consumes, saves and re-invests.

2. The social responsibilities of business extend beyond the business community and as such they should be enduring (abiding or continuing) to

(a) Play their proper role in civic affairs within the zones of the business;

(b) Promote amenities and help create better living conditions.

(c) Help in making people law-abiding and improving legislation and administration in municipal and industrial affairs; and

(d) Set up socially desirable standards of living themselves, ostentatious (conspicuous), wasteful and improvident expenditure in weddings, festivities and parties.

3. Business owes it to itself as a primary obligation, to give fair and square deal to its customers and consumers. They should be charged a fair and reasonable price which should be well within their reach. The supply of goods should be of uniform standard, and of reasonably good quality. The distribution of goods must be so widespread as to be within the reach of the consumer. No business should directly or indirectly indulge in profiteering, hoarding or creating artificial scarcity.

4. Business should not mislead the consumer and community by false, misleading and exaggerated advertisements. Obscene (vulgar) advertisements are demoralizing and a danger to public morals.

5. Business should develop its administration in such a way as to promote a spirit of co-operative endeavour between employers and employees. There should be a sense of participation between the capital on the one hand and labour and skill on the other in their objective towards prosperity and progress.

6. Business should endeavour to pay -

(a) Fair and reasonable wages to its labour,

(b) Fair and reasonable remuneration and salaries to its staff

(c) Fair and reasonable return to themselves for their work and capital without creating unseemly disparities and by providing fair and reasonable progress and promotion within the business administration from one level to another.

7. Business should develop and adopt a progressive labour policy based on -

(a) Recognition of genuine trade union rights, settlement of disputes and conciliation.

(b) Participation of the workers in improving production and administration.

(c) Creating a sense of their belonging to the business and

(d) Improving the human qualities of labour by education, training, living-conditions, housing and amenities.

8. The social responsibilities of business include a healthy co-operative inter-business relationship between different businesses and avoidance of such unfair practices as price rigging, undercutting, patronage, unfair canvassing and unethical advertisements.

9. The social responsibilities of business towards the State demand that -

(a) The businessman will be a law-abiding citizen.

(b) He will pay his dues and taxes to the state fully and honestly,

(c) He will not corrupt public servants and the democratic processes for his selfish ends,

(d) He will not buy political support by money or patronage,

(e) He will sell his commodities and services without adulteration,

(f) He will maintain a fair trade policy and avoid activities leading to restraint of trade.

Business community must read the writing on the wall and take without delay, appropriate steps to regulate its conduct and cultivate self-discipline and self-regulation in the larger national interests. In the current Indian context, business cannot hope to survive unless it faces the realities and fulfil both its economic as well as its social roles. This is not merely for protecting the interest of consumers but also to protect its own interest. Therefore, today, businessmen can do their business only with public acceptability; otherwise they will have no business left to transact.

BUSINESS ETHICS IN INDIA

Profit in any business is not a crime, it is essential for survival and growth. However, illegal profit through questionable means like product adulteration, fraud, manipulation, supply of short weights and measures deceptive packaging, unethical advertising, misbranding, inflationary price practices such as hoarding, black-marketing and so on are considered both anti-social and anti-national.

There has been a lot of concern expressed about the unethical practices being followed in India. A business may commit unethical practices against the consumers, employees, community and Government. They include:

1. With reference to Consumers -
   - (a) Adulteration.
   - (b) Lack of safety regulation.
   - (c) Short weights and measures.
   - (d) Spurious products.
   - (e) Duplicates.
   - (f) Injurious products.
   - (g) Unethical and deceptive advertisement.
2. With reference to Employees -
   - (a) Low salaries
   - (b) Poor working conditions
3. With reference to Government and Community -
   - (a) Tax evasion.
   - (b) Pollution.

1. Unethical Practices Against Consumers

(a) Adulteration: Food adulteration is so rampant in India, that the consumers do not get wholesome or right quality and quantity of food. There have been reports of adulteration to the extent that may cause serious health problems. In India, adulteration has assumed a commercial character. Adulteration is remarkable and very handy way for any businessmen to get rich quickly. In the bargain, it is the innocent masses of people who are the losers. Everything is adulterated today. It is estimated that 30% of all food items are adulterated in India. Adulteration to the extent that it may take the lives of consumers has not been uncommon.

(b) Lack of Safety Regulations: Numerous sophisticated products are being used by consumers in their daily life such as flammable fabrics, cooking stoves, electrical appliances and many other hazardous products. Due to want of adequate information on safety measures, hundreds of men, women and children have died of fires and accidents.

(c) Short Weights and Measures: The consumer's hard earned money is simply lost due to short weights alone. Sample surveys of markets have shown that more than 80% of the purchases made are underweight. This survey has highlighted the enormous loss to consumers by the use of short weights and measures.

(d) Spurious Products: Some businessmen have done to the extent of selling spurious products. There are so many spurious or bogus cosmetics and medicines in the market playing havoc with the lives and money of the public. Backyard factories have been found producing antibiotics and other potent and dangerous drugs of doubtful quality. Even life-saving medicines have not been spared.

(e) Duplicates: Many popular goods are subject to imitation manufacture. Detergents, soft-drinks, jams, oils and other products are duplicated and sold under popular brand names. Many of the duplicate products are of doubtful quality and are even injurious to the user.

(f) Injurious Products: Products which have been proved to be health hazards are manufactured and sold purely for commercial gains. There are cosmetics and medicines in the market playing havoc with the lives and money of the public. Backyard factories have been found producing medicines and cosmetics which are injurious to the users. Further, products injurious to health of the users like charas, marijuana etc., are sold for purely commercial gains.

(g) Unethical and Deceptive Advertisements: Misleading advertisements can be found on bill boards, in newspapers, T.V., Radio and other mass media channels. In these advertisements, highly pampered statements are used about the products. Consumers are tempted to buy on the basis of false advertisements. Advertisements of wonder drugs blatantly proclaiming magic remedy and solving all problems of health, wealth, love, marriage etc., is not uncommon today. Many creams, which might actually spoil one's beauty, are propagated as beauty creams. Drinks that hardly contribute to one's health are marketed as health drinks. One glaring malpractice about infant foods is given as an example. Breast-feeding is cleverly discouraged and large companies give free gifts etc. to promote infant foods. Because of this high pressure advertising, ignorant mothers turn away from breast-feeding and are encouraged to give artificial infant food. Innumerable low income families, were systematically induced to discard breast feeding and adopt artificial infant food which these low income families could not afford and which they were unable to prepare in the right strength and with proper sterilization because most of the mothers were illiterate and ignorant. Thus, mother's milk which is best for infants, since it was safe, hygienic and nutritious is discarded because of unethical and deceptive advertisement promoting bottle-feeding. This is both immoral and unethical.

2. With reference to Employees

(a) Low Salaries: Wages in the widest sense mean any economic compensation paid by the employer under some contract to workers for the services rendered by them. Salaries paid to the employees tend to be very low especially in a country like India where labour is in abundance. The wages paid to workers should be adequate to enable an employee to maintain himself and his family at a reasonable level of existence. However, employers do not generally favour using

the concept of a living wage as a guide to wage determination because they prefer to pay on "the prevailing market rate" which is very low. Thus, the worker's are exploited by the business through this unethical wage policy of unscrupulous businessmen.

(b) Poor Working Conditions: The life of industrial workers is full of risks and hazards. The risk and hazard is the result of some unsafe work conditions, defective plant or shop lay out, inadequate ventilation, unsafe and insufficient lighting arrangements or insufficient space for movement inside the plant or shop. But employers hardly pay any attention to the work environment. They consider providing better working conditions as unnecessary expenses which can be best avoided. This is a sad state of affairs because working conditions tend to be unhygienic - inadequate ventilation, poor lighting, no welfare facilities besides safety of the workers is not cared for since workers spend about eight hours on a working day at their work-place, they must be provided with good working conditions. Good working conditions are necessary to maintain the health of the workers.

3. With Reference to Government and Community

Every business owes an obligation towards the Government and the society at large. It is the duty of the business to manage its affairs according to the law affecting it. The specific responsibilities of the business to the Government and the community are given below:

(a) Tax Evasion: Every business should pay taxes and other government dues honestly, fully and promptly. One of the basic reasons of tax evasion is the high rate of taxation. However, it is doubtful, if lower rates of taxation will make the business men more sincere towards the Government. It must be stated here that the business community must endeavour to pay the taxes as social development is possible

only if the government has the revenue. In fact, the high rate of taxation is the result of tax evasion.

(b) Pollution: Every business should take preventive measures against water and air pollution. The organization has the responsibility to keep the environment free from pollution. In fact, pollution is one of the major unethical practices being followed by business. If the business fails to discharge its responsibilities, the government will interfere to prevent the enterprise from spoiling the environment.

PROFESSIONALISATION OF MANAGEMENT

There has been a growing trend towards professionalisation of management. Professionalisation imparts a certain social responsibility and dignity to management. A professional cannot be controlled or directed by the client. He has professional knowledge and judgment which he uses to make his decision. Thus, professionalisation makes business more efficient, dynamic and socially responsible. The growth of management education in India has contributed to professionalisation in the business field.

The company form of business organization which has split ownership from management and the gaining popularity of the company form of business organization have increased the need for professional managers.

Is management a profession? To answer this question, first of all we should understand what a profession is. Many authorities on the subject have attempted to define a profession. According to Abraham Flexner, A profession is -

1. A body of specialized knowledge and recognized educational process of acquiring it.
2. A standard of qualifications governing admission to the profession.
3. A standard of conduct governing the relationship of

the practitioners with clients, colleagues and the public.

4. An acceptance of the social responsibility inherent in an occupation and the public interest.
5. An association or society devoted to the advancement of the social obligations as distinct from the economic interests of the group.

According to Lewis Allen, " a professional manager is one who specializes in the work of planning, organizing, leading and controlling the efforts of others and does so through a systematic use of classified knowledge, a common vocabulary and principles, who subscribes to the standards of practice and code of ethics established by a recognized body".

According to Peter Drucker, "Professional management is a function, a discipline, a task to be done; and managers are the professionals who practice this discipline, carry out the functions and discharge these tasks. It is no longer relevant whether the manager is also an owner; if he is it is incidental to his main function, which is to be a manager."

The World Council of Management has recommended the following criteria for professionalisation. They are -

1. Members of a profession subordinate self-interest to the client interest and the official interest.
2. A profession is based on a systematic body of knowledge that is held to common and lends to application.
3. Membership of a profession should depend on the observance of certain rules of conduct or behaviour.

A critical evaluation of the above definitions show that professionalisation of business management shows that -

1. There exists a systematic body of knowledge on management. A professional should have formally acquired the specialized knowledge and skill for management. Management is taught as a discipline in various educational institutes, throughout the world.
2. Membership of a profession should depend on the observance of certain rules of conduct and behaviour. The decisions and actions of a professional are guided by certain ethical considerations.
3. A profession is based on a systematic body of knowledge that is held in common and lends itself to application. Thus, a profession should have no ideological bias in the discharge of his functions.

A close scrutiny of management shows that management unlike law or medicine is not a full-fledged profession. The reasons are -

1. It is not obligatory to possess specific qualifications for being appointed as a manager.
2. There is no single association to regulate the educational and training standards of managers.
3. Uniform professional standards have not been set up for the practicing managers.

Thus, from the above mentioned discussion we can understand that management fulfill certain criteria to call it a profession. Whereas, it fails to meet certain other criteria, therefore, we can conclude that management is not a full fledged profession but it is advancing towards professionalisation.

QUESTIONS
(For Self-Study)

1. What is meant by social responsibility of business? How can a modern business discharge its social responsibility?
2. What is meant by business ethics? Why should a business make ethical decisions?
3. What are the responsibilities that business owes to the consumers, society and Government?
4. Explain the different types of business ethics.

UNIVERSITY QUESTIONS

(5 Marks)

- Narrate the role of trade association in the promotion of Business Ethics.(October/November 2004)
- Mention the important ethical principles that a business should follow... (April 2004)
- In what way trade associations can promote business ethics (October 2003)
- What is Business Ethics? Which are the important ethical principles that a business should follow? (April/May 2003) (October 2003)
- Which are the important ethical principles that a business should follow? (April/May 1997)

(1 Mark)

- Business ethics (October 2003)

3

INDIAN ECONOMIC ENVIRONMENT

Learning Objectives

After going through this chapter, you will be conversant with:

- Capitalism
  1. Features
  2. Advantages
  3. Disadvantages
- Socialism
  1. Features
  2. Advantages
  3. Disadvantages
- Mixed Economy
  1. Features
  2. Advantages
  3. Disadvantages
     - Brief history of the Indian economy
     - Nature of an underdeveloped economy
     - Indian economy as an underdeveloped economy
     - Indian Socialism
     - Economic rules of the Government

The economic conditions of a country are very important determinants of business strategies. The nature of the economy, the stage of development of the economy, economic resources etc., are the important determinants affecting the business.

The scope of private business activities depend to a large extent on the nature of the economic system. The term "economic system" refers to "the orderly arrangement or organization pattern formed by a set of various institutions and bodies governing the economic activities - production, distribution, exchange, consumption and growth - in a community".

According to Prof. Loucks and Whitney " an economic system consists of those institutions which a given people or nation or group of nations has chosen or accepted through their resources are utilized for the satisfaction of human wants". The forms of economic activities depend upon the type of economic system. The major forms of economic systems are

(1) Capitalism

(2) Socialism and

(3) Mixed Economy.

The general features of these three distinctive economic systems are discussed below.

1. CAPITALISM

A Capitalist economic system is a market-oriented economy in which the resources of production are owned by the private individuals. The interference of the government in the functioning of the economic-system is the minimum.

According to Gary M Pickergill and Joyce E Pickergill - "The Capitalist system is one characterized by the private ownership of the means of production, individual decision making and the use of the market mechanism to carry out the decision of individual participants and facilitate the flow of goods and services in markets".

The Capitalist system is also known as free enterprise economy and market economy.

Characteristic Features of Capitalism

The important characteristic features of capitalist system are:

1. *Limited Role of Government:* The Government does not play any role in a private enterprise economy. This system is a highly idealized system. There is hardly any pure capitalist system in the real world today. Government intervention is necessary to ensure smooth functioning of the capitalist system. Government interference is necessary to protect property rights, enforce contractual agreements and ensure the satisfaction of certain community wants.

2. *Private Ownership*: The factors of production like land, labour and capital are privately owned in a capitalist economy. Individuals are free to use their property as they like as long as they do not infringe on the rights of others. The concept of private property is protected, controlled and enforced by law. Production therefore occurs at private initiative. Capitalism confers full fledged right of private ownership of productive resources in private hands.

3. *Market System:*. The market mechanism is the pivot on which the wheels of a capitalistic economy turns. A market economy is one in which buyers and sellers decide how much they are willing to pay for or how much they demand of goods and services. The price system is regarded as the organizing force in a capitalist economy. Therefore, the market mechanism is the key factor that regulates the capitalist economy.

4. *Free Enterprise:* The term free enterprise implies that the private firms are allowed to obtain resources, organize production and sell the resultant products in any way the

firm chooses. In other words, there will be least government interference on the freedom and ability of private individuals in carrying out business. Free enterprise is an essential feature of capitalism.

5. *Consumer's Sovereignty:* "Consumers are the kings" under capitalism. In a capitalist economy the consumer rights are well protected and consumers have the right to choose from the different alternatives. There exists a buyers market and the sellers will give royal treatment to all the buyers. The production decisions in the free market economy are based on the consumer desires which are reflected in the demand pattern.

6. *Competition:* Competition is the most essential feature of a capitalist economy. The competition reduces the imperfections in the market and results in the consumer sovereignty. It offers the best possible services to the consumers. Competition among sellers and buyers is an essential feature of an ideal capitalist system. Competition is necessary in a capitalistic economy to keep initiative constantly on the alert, maintain flexible price system and to protect the consumers.

7. *Freedom of choice of Occupation*: In a capitalist economy, every individual has the right to take up the occupation that he feels right for him. The freedom of choice enables the employees to put forth their terms and conditions to the employers. This freedom of choice of occupation implies the employers have to competitively bid for labour.

8. *Freedom to Save and Invest:* In a capitalistic economy, people enjoy the right of savings and investing the same in investment projects they feel the best. The freedom to save, and accumulate wealth is a distinguishing feature of the private enterprise system.

9. *Absence of a Central Plan:* The activities of economic

units are not guided, co-ordinate or controlled by a central plan. Resource allocation and investment decisions are influenced by market forces without interference by the State. Therefore, the capitalist system is characterized by the absence of a central plan.

10. Profit Oriented: Production in a capitalist economy is always "profit oriented". Resource allocation and investment decisions are influenced by profits. Thus, capitalist are guided and controlled by the profits they hope to make.

Demerits of Capitalism

The capitalistic system has the following demerits.

1. Profitability criterion for investment: A large part of the resources of the nation are utilized for the satisfaction of the needs of the rich. This is so because investment allocation is guided by the profitability criterion. Therefore, sufficient investment may not take place in areas where profitability is low, however essential they may be. Thus, we can say that capitalistic system is pro-rich and anti-poor.

2. Unequal distribution of income and wealth: The right to property are likely to lead to concentration of income and wealth in the hands of a few capitalists. This will lead to the widening of income disparities. Therefore it is said that the capitalistic system makes the rich richer and poor poorer. The result is the bad effects of class conflicts etc.

3. Scope for Cut-throat Competition: Free competition will give scope for cut throat competition. Large firms are likely to gain an advantageous position which would ultimately lead to monopolies.

2. SOCIALISM

Socialism is generally understood as an economic system where the means of productions are either owned or controlled by the State. Under such a system, the resource allocation, investment pattern, consumption and distribution patterns etc., are directed and regulated by the state. Socialism evolved as a remedial measure to correct the evils of capitalism.

According to Dickinson, "Socialism is an economic organization of the society in which the material-means of production are owned by the whole community or State and operated by organs and representatives of and responsible to the community according to a general economic plan, all members of the community are entitled to benefit from the result of such socialized planned production on the basis of equal rights."

Characteristic Features of Socialism

The characteristic features of a socialist system are:

1. *Government Ownership and Control:* Under socialism the means of production are either owned or controlled by the State. In some socialist economies, the private sector also plays a very small role. However, the Government directs and regulates investment allocation in accordance with national priorities. Thus, we can say that in socialist countries, the major means of production are either owned by the Government or their use is controlled by the Government. When the state owns almost the whole of the means of production and controls the private sector, it is much easier to achieve the desired pattern of resource allocation.

In communist countries like Russia and China, the means of production are mostly owned by the state.

2. *Central Authority:* The socialist economies generally have a central authority which will determine the policy for exploitation, utilization and distribution of economic resources. They are also called command economies because the central planning authority decides the pattern of resource utilization.

3. *Distribution of Income:* A Socialist country aims at equality in income distribution. Equality in income distribution does not mean the equal distribution of income. It refers to the removal of the huge gap between the incomes of the rich and the poor. An equitable distribution of income is an important feature of the socialist system. Wage differentials are recognized but they are kept at a minimum in socialistic countries.

4. *Fixation of wages and prices:* The wage rates and prices in a socialist country is fixed by the government and not by the market forces. Therefore, the sellers will not be in a position to determine their own prices for the sale of goods and services.

5. *Restriction on Occupation:* Individual freedom of enterprise is absent. Similarly the freedom of occupation is also absent or restricted in socialist countries. A citizen of a socialistic country does not have the freedom to choose his own occupation.

6. *Restriction on Consumption:* In socialistic countries, consumer sovereignty is absent. The state decides what may be made available to consumers. The consumers have the freedom to choose from the narrow variety that the state makes available to him. Thus the consumers in a socialistic country have to be content with the variety provided to him by the State.

Advantages of Socialism

Socialism has its own merits or advantages. They are -

1. Equality of income and wealth.
2. Scope for rational socio-economic decisions of the Government.

3. A planned adjustment of resources to cater to the needs of the society in contrast to the needs of the individual as in the case of capitalistic countries.
4. Since socialistic economies are command economies the planning authority plans the pattern of resource utilization, therefore, there is absence of economic exploration, trade cycles etc.
5. There is wide scope for optimum utilization of the scarce resources and for the maximization of social welfare in a socialistic economy.
6. The socialist economies generally have a central authority to formulate the national plan, it is possible to achieve a rapid economic progress.

Disadvantages of Socialism

Socialism has its disadvantages or demerits also. They are -

1. *Undue Government Control:* The Government directs and regulates investment allocation and production pattern. This undue Government interference restricts the growth of the private enterprise. In fact, socialistic countries like China have now understood its mistakes and have opened its doors not only to private capitalists to foster development.

2. *Restricted Individual Freedom:* In a socialistic country there is restriction to the freedom of choosing any occupation. This restriction will kill the initiative among the people.

3. *Absence of Consumer Sovereignty:* In a socialistic country there is no consumer sovereignty because the state decided what may be made available to consumers. Therefore the consumers have to be content with what the state provides for them.

3. MIXED ECONOMY

The mixed economy, shares certain features of private capitalism and state capitalism. It is a blending of capitalism and socialism. Mixed economy is characterized by the co-existence of public sector and private sector. A mixed economy tries to combine all the best features of capitalism and socialism and attempts to avoid the demerits or limitations of both the systems.

A mixed economy may therefore be defined as, "an economy in which resources are allocated and exploited partly through the decisions of private individuals and firms and partly through the decisions of the Government and State owned enterprises".

Features of Mixed Economy

A mixed economic system has the following distinguished features:

1. Participation of both public sector and private sector in the economic development of the economy.
2. Greater emphasis on social welfare than on personal welfare.
3. Inevitability of economic-planning with a democratic approach.
4. Equal scope for both public and private sectors.

Advantages of a Mixed Economy

A mixed economic system has the following advantages or merits. They are:

1. Healthy competition between private and public sectors.
2. Scope for private initiative as there is the right of private property in a mixed economy.

3. There is full scope for creativity, personal freedom and economic liberty.
4. A mixed economy has a inbuilt mechanism for social-justice, economic equality and improved standard of living of the people.

Disadvantages of a Mixed Economy

A mixed economy suffers from certain limitations. They are -

1. Over-emphasis of government role and of public-sector undertakings.
2. Conflicting ideas of socialism and capitalism.
3. Frequent economic fluctuations and high inflationary pressures.

BRIEF HISTORY OF THE INDIAN ECONOMY

Indian Economy in the Pre-British Period

The economic conditions in India during the pre-British period were almost similar to those which prevailed in most of the European countries. The agricultural sector and industrial sector were satisfactory while trade and transport were just satisfactory. The Indian economy consisted of self-sustaining villages. The village community was based on a simple division of labour. There were three distinct classes in villages.

(1) The agriculturists

(2) The village artisans like goldsmiths, weavers, carpenters, potters, washermen, blacksmith etc.,

(3) The village officials, money lenders, landlords, etc.

Most of the food produced in the village was consumed by the village population itself. The raw materials produced from agriculture were used by the handicraft industry. Thus the interdependence of agriculture and handicraft industry provided the basis of the village to function independently of the outside world. Labour and Capital needed was either supplied by the producers themselves or by the village land lord or by the village money lender. The villages however suffered from aggressors and were forced to submit to exactions, plunder and extortions.

Though India was predominantly an agricultural economy, Indian industries enjoyed a worldwide reputation. The chief industry was textile industry. The Dacca muslin, Banaras saris and other cotton fabrics were well known to the foreigners. India was also quite well known for her artistic industries like marble-work, stone-carving, Wood-carving, jewellery etc. Thus, Indian exports consisted chiefly of manufacturers like cotton and silk fabrics, pepper, opium, indigo etc.

British Rule in India

India was under British rule between 1757 and 1947. The British rule can be divided into two categories. The first category is the rule of the British East Indian Company from 1757 to 1858. The second category is the rule of the British Crown from 1858 to 1947.

Indian culture, administration and economy have been largely influenced by the British. Whatever little advancement India had at the time of independence was due to the pioneering efforts of the British administrators combined with the efforts of British capitalist and a few Indians. The British administration in India ensured the unity, safety and security which are important for the development of any economy. The growth of railways, the development of Post and Telegraph, the spread of irrigation and the expansion of education were the important contribution of British rule in India.

Before the beginning of Industrial Revolution in England, the British East India Company exported Indian textiles, spices etc., to Europe. The Industrial Revolution reversed this. Tremendous expansion of productivity capacity of British Industries resulted in increased demand for raw materials for British Industries and the need to capture foreign markets. Therefore, the British policy changed and their aim now was to exploit India's natural resources for the benefit of British Industries. The four important consequences for the Indian economy due to the British rule are:

1. Decline of Indian handicrafts and ruralisation of the economy.
2. Introduction of new land system.
3. Commercialization of agriculture.
4. The process of industrial transition.

1. Decline of Handicrafts and Ruralisation of the Indian Economy: The industrial revolution in Great Britain resulted in tremendous expansion of productive capacity of British Industry. This resulted in increased demand for raw materials for British industry and the need to capture foreign markets. Therefore steps were taken to commercialize agriculture so that the export of raw materials could be stepped up. Efforts were also made to crush Indian industries and help the process of industrialization of Britain. The worst to be hit by this duel exploitation by the British administration in India was the textile handicrafts. The principal causes that led to the decline of handicrafts were as follows:

(a) The growth of a number of handicrafts industries was made possible because of Royal patronage of princes and rajas. British rule meant the disappearance of princes and rajahs and consequently their patronage.

(b) The Industrial Revolution in Great Britain resulted

in large-scale production and cheaper machine made goods. Indian made goods could not withstand the competition of machine made cheaper goods of Great Britain.

(c) The British were always guided by their own interests. They formulated certain policies, which helped British Industries. This selfish policy of the British Government in India crippled Indian Industries and helped the process of industrialization in Britain.

(d) With the spread of education and English culture, the upper class of Indians began to imitate British dress and fashions. Indigenous goods went out of fashion and the demand for British commodities increased. This led to a change in the pattern of demand of the people who slowly discarded Indian goods and substituting them with British goods.

The decline of Indian handicrafts resulted in unemployment on a mass scale and the displaced artisans taking up agriculture for their sustenance.

2. *Introduction of New Land System:* Another impact of the British rule is the growth of a new land system in India called the Zamindari System. Under this system land revenue was fixed and revenue collectors of the area were alleviated to the status of private land lords known as Zamindars. The Zamindars were required to deposit land revenue to the Government. The Zamindars were entitled to collect rent from the peasants. Through the introduction of Zamindary system, the British were able to create a class of people whose interests were directly tied to British rule in India. It also resulted in the creation of absentee land lords who were more interested in squeezing higher land rents than in real agricultural progress. This system, thus depressed agriculture and the peasantry.

3. *Commercialization of Agriculture:* Commercialization of agriculture implies production of crops for sale rather than for family consumption. During the British rule, Indian agriculture was commercialized to cater to the needs of the British industries for necessary raw materials. This led to a phenomenal fall in the production of food crops because, peasants shifted to industrial crops. These factors retarded the process of industrialization in the country.

4. *Process of Industrial Transition:* The process of Industrial transition under the British rule was mainly in the private sector. It took mainly two forms, viz., plantation and factory. Organized industry on a large scale was introduced in India only by the British. The British had experience of running industries therefore; it was but natural that they pioneered industrial enterprise in India. Indians in the early days were unfamiliar with the conduct of modern business enterprises and the indigenous capital was not forthcoming due to lack of technical know how. They invested their capital in plantation, factories and mining. India integrated itself with world capitalism during the British rule. The ancient handicrafts were destroyed to make way for machine made goods of the British. A close look at the economic development reveals that a paradoxical transition of modernization with underdevelopment had taken place in India.

Thus, the Indian economy presented a dual picture of modernization and underdevelopment when India got independence in 1947. However, after independence, India has started marching towards the goal of a developed economy with the launching of five year plans starting from 1951.

NATURE OF AN UNDERDEVELOPED ECONOMY

Definition

It is not easy to define an under-developed economy.

However, different economists have attempted to define underdeveloped economy.

Jacob Venir defines an underdeveloped country as "a country which has good potential prospects for using more capital or more labour or more available natural resources or all of these to support its present population on a higher level of living or if its per capita income level is already fairly high to support a larger population on a not lower level of living."

According to Prof Rangar Nurkse - "Underdeveloped Countries are those which compared with the advanced countries, are under-equipped with capital in relation to their population and natural resources".

Eugene Staley defines an underdeveloped country as "A country characterized by (i) mass poverty which is chronic and not the result of some temporary misfortune and (ii) obsolete methods of production and social organization, which means that the poverty is not due to poor natural resources and hence could presumably be lessened by methods already proved in other countries".

Oskar Lange defines - "an underdeveloped economy as an economy in which the stock of capital goods available is not sufficient to employ the available labour force on the basis of modern techniques of production".

Features

The above definitions of an underdeveloped economy bring out the following features. They are -

1. Underdeveloped economies are distinguished from the developed economies on the basis of the low per capita income. Per Capita income is the most significant measure of comparison.

2. Mass poverty is the most important problem of an underdeveloped economy. Mass poverty is the main cause of low level of development.
3. Mass poverty in underdeveloped countries is not due to poor natural resources, but is the consequence of obsolete method of production and exploitative social structure.
4. The low resource base of the poor also inhibits them from giving education to their children. Therefore, the children of the poor are either engaged in unskilled occupations or some semi-skilled occupations. This enables them to earn very low and meagre (insufficient) wages and thus perpetuates mass poverty.

INDIAN ECONOMY AS AN UNDER-DEVELOPED ECONOMY

India is an underdeveloped economy. Judging from any standard, India is an underdeveloped economy. A bulk of its population lives in conditions of poverty and misery. Poverty is not only acute but is also a chronic malady. We give below some important characteristics of an under-developed economy to prove the fact that India is an underdeveloped country.

1. Low Per Capita Income: Underdeveloped economies are marked by the existence of low per capita income. Baring a few countries in the world, the per capita income of the Indian people is the lowest in the world. Underdeveloped countries have been generally identified on the basis of the level of their per capita income being less than 1/5th of the per capita income of the United States of America. The per capita income of an Indian in 1991 was $330. Not only in the per capita income in India is very low, it is increasing at a very slow rate when compared to other developed countries. This has widened the gap between the two.

2. *Low Standard of Living:* As a result of low per capita income quite a substantial proportion of the population is poor. Those below the poverty line are unable to meet even the minimum calorie needs of their physical existence. The acuteness of the poverty is thus more obvious from the low level of consumption of these people.

3. *Occupational Pattern is predominantly agriculture:* One of the basic characteristics of an underdeveloped economy is that it is primary producing. According to Colin Clerk and Keeznets, economic development consists in progressive enlargement of the proportion of tertiary occupations. The underdeveloped economies, on the other hand, are such in which primary occupations predominate. India's national income, to a large extent, is derived from agriculture. In India, in 1981, about 71% of the working population was engaged in agriculture and its contribution to national income was 36%. According to the 1991 census, 65% of India's working population was engaged in agriculture. This excessive dependence on agriculture is due to the fact that non-agricultural occupations have not grown at a rate commensurate with the increase in population owing to lack of sufficient investment outside agriculture. Thus, India's economy in essence is an agrarian economy.

4. *Under-Utilization of Natural Resources:* The natural resources in an underdeveloped economy are either unutilised or under-utilized. The hidden natural resources have not been fully explored at all. Even known resources remain unutilised or under utilized on account of the inaccessibility of natural resources, lack of capital, technological knowledge, skill etc. The natural resources of India remain still largely underdeveloped. Vast natural resources like forest and mineral wealth remain unexplored. Therefore, it is rightly observed that India is a rich country inhabited by poor people. What this means is that India has many resources and is therefore

a rich country in this sense. But the resources are not fully utilized for the production of material goods and services, hence the people are poor.

5. *Population Explosion:* India's population is very large. According to the 1991 census India's population is more than 84 crores. The fast rate of growth of population necessitates a higher rate of economic growth in order to maintain the same standard of living of the population. The main problem in India is the high level of birth rates coupled with a falling level of death rates. The rate of growth of population during 1981-92 is about 2.11 per cent. To maintain a rapidly growing population, the requirements of food, clothing, shelter, schooling, medicine etc all raise. Thus, a raising population imposes greater economic burdens and consequently, the country has to make a much greater effort to initiate the process of growth. Moreover, a raising population leads to an increase in labour force leading to unemployment.

6. *Prevalence of chronic unemployment:* Less developed countries are characterized by large unemployment and underemployment both of which have been chronic and largely rural. One important consequence, of this rapid rate of population growth is that it throws more and more people on land to eke out their living from agriculture, since alternative occupations do not simultaneously develop at that rapid rate and thus are not there to absorb the increasing numbers seeking gainful employment. The resultant pressure of population on land thus gives raise to disguised unemployment.

In India, labour is an abundant factor and consequently, it is very difficult to provide gainful employment to the entire work force. On the other hand, in developed countries unemployment is of a cyclical nature and occurs due to lack of effective demand. Thus, we can say that in India unemployment is structural and is the result of deficiency of capital. The Indian economy does not find sufficient capital to expand its industries to such an extent that the entire labour force is absorbed. The total unemployed during the eighth plan are estimated to be 65 million. The existence of unemployment of this magnitude is a matter of serious concern.

7. Capital Deficiency and the Low rate of Capital formation: The basic characteristic of the Indian economy is the existence of capital deficiency i.e., the amount of capital per head is low and further to increase the problem, the current rate of capital formation is also low. This low capital stock is not adequate for equipping well the entire labour force for the full utilization of natural resources. According to Professor Colin Clark, in order to maintain the same level of living a country requires an additional investment of 4% per annum, for a 1% per annum increase in population growth. Therefore, for 2.11% increase in population an investment of 8% is needed to offset the additional burden imposed by a raising population. Therefore, in order to improve living standard of the population and to pave the way for economic growth a still higher rate of capital formation is required. So, in the context of the raising population, the present rate of capital formation is not adequate.

8. Poor Quality of Human Capital: A glaring feature of an underdeveloped economy is the poor quality of human capital. The position in respect of human capital depends on education, training, health facilities etc. In India, the poor quality of human capital can be judged by the high rate of illiteracy and the inadequacy of health facilities. A minimum level of education is necessary to acquire skills and also to comprehend social problems. According to the 1991 census, 48% of the population is illiterate whereas in advanced countries illiteracy is 0% to 5%. In respect of health too the facilities in our country are grossly short of requirements.

9. Prevalence of low level of Technology: Almost all the underdeveloped countries are dual economies. In India, the most modern technique exists side by side with the most primitive in the same industry. But the majority of the productive units and a major part of the output is produced with the help of traditional inferior techniques.

10. Poor Economic Organization: In the Indian economy, certain institutions necessary for economic development are not adequately developed. India suffers from inadequacy of financial institutions especially in rural areas. The development of financial institutions for mobilizing savings and also for granting credit to farmers is needed. Likewise, the development of industrial finance corporations is also quite necessary.

To conclude, we can say that even after more than four decades of planning, India continues to exhibit the basic characteristics of an underdeveloped economy. Poverty is writ large on the faces of masses of India. However, India has progressed substantially in certain areas.

Causes of Underdevelopment of the Indian Economy

It has been argued that the economic backwardness is a direct consequence of the paucity of resources. But India has been blessed with vast resources and most of these resources remain either unutilized or under-utilized. Thus it makes little sense to explain India's backwardness in terms of paucity of resources. It is said that the backwardness of the Indian economy is the consequence of various factors. They are -

1. Economic Factors: The lack of capital is a major factor for the economic backwardness of India. Even the little capital that is available is invested unproductively or is simply hoarded in the form of cash or jewellery. Thus, capital goods are at an absolute minimum and are even insufficient for the production of even essential goods. From the stand point of economic development capital is an important component which the Indian Economy very much lacks.

2. *Political Factors:* Under the British rule, India did develop a stable and strong government but very little effort was made to promote the economic development of India. Industrial and commercial policies were so designed that not only the new industries were prevented from coming up but also the existing manufacturing industries were destroyed. The growth of the economy in the post-independence period is however, several times better than what was achieved during the first half of the 20th century under British rule. The role of the state, therefore, emerges as the single most dominant factor affecting economic development.

3. *Technological Backwardness:* As a result of backward technology there is low productivity of labour as well as capital. Backward technology is a cause of economic backwardness.

4. *Institutional Deficiencies:* It has been argued that certain institutional deficiencies are responsible for economic backwardness. In India, the banking system is not fully developed. Even today, India does not possess a sufficient number of industrial and agricultural banks. Further, India does not have a fully developed capital market. These deficiencies have made the mobilization of capital and its proper investment a very difficult task. Besides poor banking and financial institutions, transport, communication and power resources are also underdeveloped and are an important factor for the backwardness of the Indian economy.

5. *Social Factors:* India's underdevelopment is also due to her religious and social structure. In India, there are religious customs, practices and social institutions like cast system, the joint family system etc which foster attitudes which are inimical to economic growth. Belief in life after death, the hereditary character of many occupations, restrictions on mobility, lack of interest in worldly material life etc are cited as some of the drawbacks in the Indian people.

INDIAN SOCIALISM

Mixed economy is a compromise between laissez-faire and socialization. The classicists believed that economic liberty was the key-note for all economic progress. They also believed in self-sustaining nature of economic system, self-interest, free play of supply and demand etc. After the First World War the ideas of classicists began to lose its importance. Laissez faire failed to maintain full-employment and economic system was incapable of self-adjustment. The great depression called for some immediate action to set things in perfect order. It was argued that the alternative was consisted in the complete socialization of means of production. But Keynes opposed the complete socialization of means of production. Instead he favoured a compromise between the two extremes i.e., Government participation along with individual enterprise in economic sphere. His advice was translated into the economic policies of the governments in many countries. India was one of the many countries. Thus we have reached the concept of "mixed Economy".

Thus, India has adopted neither pure Capitalism nor Perfect Socialism. It has restored to a mixed economy form of economic system. Therefore, unlike capitalist economies and socialist countries we find the operation of public sector and private sector together in the Indian economy. Following are the important features of Indian socialism.

1. *It is neither Capitalism nor Socialism:* Indian socialism is not characterized by the features of capitalism and socialism. It is characterized by the operation of the private sector and public sector with the interference by the State. Some of the economic activities are the exclusive areas of operation for the public sector whereas in other areas the private sector is allowed to operate. The state has undertaken the responsibility for large part of the country's industrial development and even the private sector was encouraged to function effectively.

2. *Planned Economy:* Indian economy is a planned economy which is administered and controlled with the help of the plans and policies of the State. Thus, the economic development of the country is facilitated by the five year plans, yearly plans, industrial policy statements, Industrial licensing policies etc. Thus, though entrepreneurs enjoy freedom of occupation, their activities should be subject to the state plans and policies.

3. *Removal of inequalities in wealth distribution:* Indian socialism aims at removing the maldistribution of wealth among people. Accordingly, all the state plans and policies are aimed at ensuring the distribution of wealth in such a manner that it does not result in the concentration of economic power in the hands of a few.

4. *Socialistic Pattern of Society:* The object of the Indian economy is the establishment of a socialistic pattern of society where in no distinction shall be made between individuals on the basis of race, religion, caste, creed sex etc. Accordingly, the government is said to be the Government of the people and by the people.

ECONOMIC ROLES OF GOVERNMENT

Different societies have evolved different economic systems along with the sets of social, political and economic institutions. In a capitalist economy, private sector provides goods and services. In this system, the government plays a limited role. On the other hand, socialist economy is determined by Government Sector. Market mechanism is assigned a very marginal role. In between these two, we have mixed economy where both private and public sectors appear in sizable proportion. At present, the concept of 'welfare state' has gained roots and almost all the states swear by it. Consequently over the centuries, there is a tremendous growth in government activities. Now a days it is common to use the term "public sector" or "government sector" to denote the activity of the government in its economic sphere. The most striking and universal phenomenon of recent years has been the rapid expansion of the government activity.

While the state control of economy is a universal phenomenon, the extent and nature of the control vary widely between nations depending upon the nature and stage of development of the economy, the behaviour of the private sector, the political philosophy, social attitudes etc.

Reasons for Governments Role in an Economy

The reasons for the Governments role are:

1. *Public Goods:* Certain goods which are essential to society might not be produced at all if they were not supplied by Government e.g.: defence, roads, etc. The demand for public goods is not specific and their benefits are not specific to the individuals. These goods could be provided only through a Government. Private enterprise cannot sell these goods. Because the individual knows that if these services are provided he will benefit from them whether he pays for it or not.

2. *Maximum efficiency of resource use:* Market mechanism may misguide the society where some necessities may not be produced in adequate prominence. E.g.: Luxury cars in the

midst of food scarcity. Due to these failures of the market, there is need for Government intervention.

3. *Stabilization activity:* From the point of view of economic stability also Government intervention is justified. Government protects the economy against fluctuations. For this purpose, it enters the field of banking, trading etc.

4. *Organization of Production:* In developing economies, entrepreneurship is often inadequate. In such cases, Government may provide initiative and improve organization of factor use.

5. *Income Distribution:* Market economy leads to inequality of income, a few persons have more income than required while others are at bare subsistence level. Therefore from the equity point of view, Government has to play an active role in the redistribution of income and wealth.

Nature of Government Activity

Government intervention may take different forms. They are:

1. *Governmental Conduct of Production:* "In order to meet the community goals, Government produces services directly. The Government also takes measures to produce certain goods, to avoid the evils of monopoly. Further more, there are certain types of public goods such as defence which should be supplied only by the Government since it cannot be produced and sold by private firms.

2. *The Subsidy Approach:* Subsidization of private producers to induce them to increase output or to undertake investment that they would not otherwise make is another method of intervention by the government e.g.: Subsidizing fertilizer producers so that they may sell the fertilizers to farmers at a cheaper rate. Close supervision is required to ensure that the subsidies are having the desired effect.

3. *Control Approach:* Another way of Government intervention is control approach. The Government controls those activities of private sector which give rise to significant external cost such as environmental pollution which may be subject to control. Further more, in the interest of the consumers the Government may discourage the production and use of harmful drugs, liquor etc. Besides these, the Government may bring certain rules to prevent monopolies, diseconomies etc.

4. *Transfer Payments:* Government also influences the pattern of distribution of income by the nature of tax structure. The more progressive the tax structure, the more equal will be the after-tax distribution. Further, the government may make the general transfer payment without specification of the use to certain category of persons e.g.: old age pensions.

QUESTIONS

(For Self Study)

1. Economic policy if India has been primarily directed to achieve a 'socialist pattern of society'. Do you agree?
2. Define 'mixed economy'. What are the characteristics of 'mixed economy'? Is India a mixed economy?
3. Mention any three features of the mixed economy as followed in India.

UNIVERSITY QUESTIONS

(15 Marks)

- Explain in brief the main contents of Indian Democratic Socialism (April/May 2003)
- "The Philosophy of Democratic Socialism is based on a total vision of society. India is an example". Elucidate.. (0ctober 2002)
- Distinguish between state capitalism and pure capitalism (April 1996)

- What is meant by State Capitalism? Narrate the various features of state capitalism. (October 1996)
- "Mixed Economy is the outcome of the compromise between the Lassie-Faire capitalism and state capitalism" – Explain the statement in the light of the mixed economy in India. (October 1996)
- Differentiate capitalism and socialism. Which one is superior in your opinion? (October/November 2004)
- What is pure capitalism? In what way it is different from modern capitalism? (April 2004)
- Explain the economic roles of Government. (April 2004)
- What is free enterprise economy? Explain its main features (October 2003)
- What is State Capitalism? Explain its features? (October 2003)

(5 Marks)

- In what way trade associations can promote business ethics (October 2003)
- What is Mixed Economy? (October 2003)
- What are the main drawbacks of State Capitalism (April/May 2003)

(1 Mark)

- State Capitalism (April/May 2003) (April 2004)
- Market Economy (April 2004)
- Socialistic Command Economy (April/May 2003)
- Market Socialism (April/May 2003)
- Distinguish between "Capitalism" and Socialism"(October 2002) (October 1996)
- Mention any four features of Indian Democratic Socialism (April 1996) (October 1996) (April / May 1997)

4

SOCIAL RESPONSIBILITY OF BUSINESS

Learning Objectives

After going through this chapter, you will be conversant with:

- Arguments in favour of Social Responsibility
- Arguments against Social Responsibility
- Obligations of business towards different segments of the society

Every individual living in the society has obligations towards society. Business men therefore have an obligation to run the business on those lines which make the business desirable from the point of view of society. Therefore, their decisions must be influenced by their obligations towards society. Traditionally, however the term business commonly referred to commercial activities aimed at making a profit for the owners. Therefore, the fundamental assumption was that profit maximization was the basic objective of every firm. Therefore some people argue that a business is an economic unit and therefore it does not have any responsibility towards society. However, this is not a right approach because it would be difficult to segregate the economic aspect from other aspects. Today, businessmen have reaffirmed their belief in the concept of "Social Responsibilities of Business". David and Blomstorm have observed that business is "a social institution, performing a social mission and having a broad influence on the way people live and work together".

One of the most revolutionary changes in capitalism over the last 50 years is the development of a "conscience". Private business which is the hard core of this economic system has realized and has been made to realize by several social, economic and political forces that it has social obligations to fulfil besides ensuring its own existence through profitable activity. Every individual living in the society has social obligations towards it. Viewed in this prospective, businessmen who are merely custodians of factors of production belonging to the society, have also an obligation to pursue those policies, to make those decisions and to the follow those lines of action which are desirable in terms of the objectives and values of the society. Business managers are also a part of the society. So their decisions must be influenced by their obligations towards the society.

There is no denying the fact that part of this realization is not genuine and takes the form of lip-service which is necessary to ensure the survival of private enterprises. But it cannot be denied also that private business does partly realize and recognize the hard reality that a privately owned firm cannot meet the challenge of socialism and allied doctrines unless it sets its house in order, changes its outlook and is prepared to play its legitimate role as an organ of society.

A careful study of the concept of social responsibility reveals that it has two different facets

1. Businessmen recognize that since they are managing an economic unit in the society, they have a broad obligation to the society with regard to matters affecting employment, availability of goods and inflation.

2. Social responsibility refers to both socio-economic and socio-human obligations of the business. It indicates a businessman's obligation to nurture and develop human values such as motivation, morale, co-operation and self-realization in work.

It may be argued by some people that business is wholly an economic unit and therefore, its responsibilities are limited only to economic aspect of general public and it must be judged by its economic performance. If this reasoning is accepted, the businessmen might be concerned with the economic costs of unemployment, but not with the loss of human dignity and social disorganization that accompany it. However, this is not right approach for it is very difficult to separate economic aspects of life from its other values. They are intermixed with each other. Social responsibility of business is not a new concept. Leading businessmen of the world have reaffirmed their belief in this concept. It affects their decisions and actions. They recognize that since they are managing an economic unit in the society, they have an obligation to the society with regard to their decisions and actions affecting social welfare.

It will be useful here to go into some of the forces and factors which have formed and persuaded businessmen to consider their responsibilities and the conditions which were favourable to the development of businessmen's concern with social responsibilities. Some of the more important among them are:

1. The threat of public regulation or public ownership.
2. The pressure of the labour movement.
3. The development of moral values and social standards applicable to businessmen.
4. The development of business education and contact with government and its problems.

5. Recognition of human factors contributing to the long run interests of the business people.
6. The development of a professional managerial class with a different motivation and point of view due to the separation of ownership from management in the corporate enterprise.
7. The increased complexity of the decision-making processes in which various points of view and devise interests are expressed.
8. The change in public opinion about the role of business in modern society.

These and a number of other social, ethical and economic forces have combined together to make business a socio-economic activity. Business is no longer a mere occupation; it is an economic institution operating in social environment - an institution that has to reconcile its short-term and long-range economic interests with the demands of the society in which it functions. Essentially it is this which gives raise to the general and specific social responsibilities of business.

ARGUMENTS IN FAVOUR OF SOCIAL RESPONSIBILITY OF BUSINESS

1. *Business is a creation of society and therefore it should respond to the demands of the society*: - Business managers are obliged to use its resources for the common good of society because the business uses resources which belong to the society. It is therefore necessary that every business enterprise should fulfil its obligations to society.

2. *The self-interest of business is best served by meeting the aspirations of society*: The long-term self-interests of the business are best served when business assumes social responsibilities. People who have good environment, education and opportunity make better employees, and customers for the

business. Hence there is a growing realization on the part of the enlightened business managers that it is in their self-interest to fulfil the aspirations of the society.

3. *To improve the public image of business*: - The business will retain the needed credibility with the public if it performs its social obligations. Good relations with workers, consumers and suppliers will lead to success of business.

4. *It is the moral thing to do*: - The social responsibilities of business managers must be proportionate to their social power. If the business managers do not assume social responsibility, their social power will be taken away by the society through government control and regulations and other measures.

ARGUMENTS AGAINST SOCIAL RESPONSIBILITY OF BUSINESS

1. *Responsibility of Government*: Welfare schemes are the sole responsibility of the government. Business should not have any relationship with welfare schemes. It is for the Government to adopt schemes and measures for the upliftment of the weaker sections of the society.

2. *Conflicting considerations of private market mechanism and social responsibility*: Private market mechanism and social responsibilities are opposite to each other and therefore a businessman will have to be guided by any one of the two considerations.

3. *Disregard of Market Mechanism*: Market mechanism is the appropriate way to allocate scarce resources to alternative use. The doctrine of social responsibility interferes with the market mechanism and results in an inappropriate way to allocate scarce resources.

4. *Arbitrary Power to Businessmen*: Businessmen will get arbitrary powers in the matter of allocation of resources in

the welfare of society. They should have no right to interfere with Governmental responsibility.

OBLIGATIONS OF BUSINESS TOWARDS DIFFERENT SEGMENTS OF THE SOCIETY

1. *Obligations towards owners or shareholders:* In the case of sole trader ship and partnership concerns, the owners can look after their interest themselves. Whereas in the case of the company, the directors have the following responsibilities towards the shareholders.

(a) *Reasonable Dividend* - shareholders are a source of funds for the company. They expect a high rate of dividend on the money invested by them and also the maximization of the value of their investment in the company.

(b) *Protection of assets* - The assets of the company are purchased with shareholders funds. Therefore the company is responsible to safeguard these assets.

(c) *Information* - It is the responsibility of the management to keep the shareholders informed about the financial position as well as the progress of the company.

2. *Obligations towards Customers*: Customer's satisfaction is the ultimate aim of all economic activity. Therefore, it is, the duty of management

(a) To make goods of the right quality available to the right people at the right time and place and at reasonable prices.

(b) The business should not indulge into unfair practices such as black marketing, hoarding, adulteration etc.

(c) To provide prompt and courteous service to customers.

(d) To handle customers grievances carefully.

(e) To distribute the goods and services properly so that the customers do not face any difficulty in purchasing them.

(f) To produce goods which meet the needs of the customer who belong to different classes, tastes and with different purchasing power.

3. *Obligations towards Employees*: Employees should be treated as human beings and their co-operation must be achieved for the realization of organizational goals. The business should fulfil the following obligations towards their employees.

(a) *Fair wages* - Business should pay reasonable salaries so that their employee's may lead a good life and satisfy their needs.

(b) *Adequate benefits* - Employees should be provided benefits like housing, insurance cover, medical facilities and retirement benefits.

(c) *Good Working Conditions* - Good working conditions are necessary to maintain the health of the workers. Therefore they must be provided with good working conditions.

(d) *Opportunity for Growth* - Business should give their employees opportunity to develop their capabilities through training and education.

(e) *Recognition of Worker's Rights* - The business should recognize the worker's right to fair wages, to form trade unions, to collective bargaining etc.

(f) *Co-operation* - The business must win the co-operation of the workers by creating the conditions in which workers are willing to put forward their best efforts towards the common goals of the business.

4. *Responsibility towards Suppliers*: The business must create healthy relations with the supplier. Management should deal with them judiciously. They should be provided with fair terms and conditions regarding price, quality, delivery of goods and payment.

5. *Obligations towards Government*: It is the duty of every business enterprise to manage its affairs according to the laws affecting it. It should pay taxes and other dues honestly. It should not encourage corruption, black marketing and other social evils. It should discourage the tendencies of concentration of economic power and monopoly and should encourage fair trade practices.

6. *Obligation towards society*: Every business owes an obligation to the society at large. The following are the important obligations of business towards society.

(a) *Socio-Economic Objectives* - A business should not indulge in any practice which is not fair from social point of view. The business should use the factors of production effectively and efficiently for the satisfaction of the needs of the society.

(b) *Employment Opportunities* - It is the responsibility of management to help increase direct and indirect employment in the area where it is functioning.

(c) *Efficient use of Resources* - The resources at the command of business belongs to the society. Therefore, the business should make the best possible use of the resources at its disposal for the well being of the society.

(d) *Business Morality* - The business should not indulge into anti-social and unfair trade practices such as adulteration, hoarding and black marketing.

(e) *Improving of local environment* - Business should take

preventive measures against water and air pollution. It can develop the surrounding area for the well being of the employees and the general public. A business can also contribute to the advancement of local amenities.

QUESTIONS

(for Self-Study)

1. "Economic goods and social obligations of business are always in conflict with each other and cannot be reconciled" - explain
2. "It is wrong to say that there is any conflict between profit objective and social obligations of business".
3. What is "social responsibility of business". Enumerate these responsibilities of a business.
4. Give arguments for and against the assumption of social responsibilities of a business.
5. Briefly discuss the obligations of business towards workers, consumers, investors and Government.
6. Explain the social responsibilities of business towards its shareholders, customers and community at large.

UNIVERSITY QUESTIONS

(15 Marks)

- What are social responsibilities of Business? Outline the specific responsibilities of business towards the society (October/November 2004)

(5 Marks)

- Which are the forces inducing a businessman to honour the social responsibility? (April 1996) (April / May 1997) (October 2003) (October/November 2004)
- What is Social Responsibility of Business (April/May 2003)
- Enumerate the principal factors which have led to the recognition of the social responsibility of Business (April 2004)
- Explain the social responsibility of business towards its employees (October 2002)

5

INDUSTRIAL POLICIES

Learning Objectives

After going through this chapter, you will be conversant with:

- Importance of Industrial Policy
- Objectives of Industrial Policy
- Industrial Policy prior to independence
- Industrial Policy Resolution of 1948
- Industrial Policy Resolution of 1956
- Industrial Policy Resolution of 1977
- Industrial Policy Resolution of 1980
- Industrial Policy Resolution of 1985
- Industrial Policy Resolution of 1990
- New Industrial Policy Resolution of 1991

The term Industrial Policy refers to the Government's policy towards the establishment of industries, their functioning and the working of their management. The pace and pattern of industrialization depends on the industrial policy. It is realized that an appropriate Industrial Policy of State intervention is a must for an economy like India. Industrial policy helps to make domestic and foreign sectors function in the manner as prescribed by the state and for the development of the country as a whole. Industrial Policy helps to regulate private sector and foreign sector. It further helps to co-ordinate the activities of private sector, public sector as well as Government sector.

IMPORTANCE OF INDUSTRIAL POLICY

A well-designed and well-implemented industrial policy is indispensable especially for a mixed economy which is also underdeveloped like India. The main reasons for the importance of industrial policy are: -

1. It is necessary to regulate the activities of the domestic and foreign sectors to fall in line with the requirements of the planned economy.
2. The Government must clearly earmark the areas in which the private sector as well as the public sector is required to operate. This is necessary for a country like India so that limited resources of the economy are put to an optimum use.
3. The operations of the private sector must suit the plan framework of the state. In order to achieve this, there must be proper regulation of the private sector.

OBJECTIVES OF INDUSTRIAL POLICY

The main objectives of the Industrial Policy are: -

- To achieve balanced development by earmarking spheres for public sector and private sector.
- To expand cottage and small-scale industries with the objective to provide more employment for the rural youth as well as development of the rural and backward areas.
- To accelerate the rate of industrialization, especially in the field of large scale and heavy industries.
- To expand and strengthen the public sector.
- To prevent the monopolies and concentration of economic power in the hands of a few individuals.

Thus, the concept of "Industrial Policy" is comprehensive

and it covers all those procedures, principles, policies, rules and regulations which control the industrial undertakings of a country and shape the pattern of industrialization. It incorporates fiscal and monetary policies, the tariff policy, labour policy and Government's attitude towards Foreign Sector, Public Sector and Private Sector. It therefore, defines the Governments attitude towards industrialization in the economy. Since Independence, the Government of India has announced its Industrial Policy's defining its attitude towards industrialization and the role of the public sector, joint sector, private sector and co-operative sector in the industrialization of the country. The Industrial Policy of the Government of India and the regulatory measures introduced to achieve the policy objectives has been criticized. The industrialists, foreign governments and international development organizations criticized the policy as too restrictive whereas, the leftists in India have criticized the policy not being restrictive and opposing the liberalization. If we look at the various industrial policies we can see that they have been restrictive until about the mid seventies. Having realized the disadvantages of the restrictive regime, in the 1980's onwards we can see that the process of liberalization has been followed.

To achieve the above-mentioned objectives, partial modifications have been introduced in the Industrial Policy from time to time to meet the changing needs of the situation. The following pages will describe in detail the Industrial Policy.

INDUSTRIAL POLICY PRIOR TO INDEPENDENCE

When India was under British Rule, the British Government in India mainly followed the policy of Laissez-faire. It was only during the two world wars the Government made a slight departure from the laissez-faire policy and supported the development of certain industries which were required to help the war effort. When India attained independence, there was a desire to advance industrially as quickly as possible. Therefore, the national Government wanted to develop a sound industrial policy in order to industrialize as quickly as possible.

INDUSTRIAL POLICY RESOLUTION 1948

When India won independence on August 15, 1947, industry in the country suffered a series of shocks and setbacks. Industrial relations were at their worst. Industrial raw materials were scarce. Capital was not moving freely into industrial channels. The production in India declined but population was increasing. Inflation was worsened by the economic upheaval of the partition of the country and the refugee rehabilitation problem. In view of the need to step up production and counter inflationary tendencies, it was essential to announce an industrial policy, which could create conditions of economic security which is very vital for economic growth. The national Government felt alarmed at the situation and convened the industries conference in December 1947. Among other things, the conference emphasized the need for a clear-cut demarcation of the private and the public sectors by the Government. In spite of its pre-occupation with a number of other problems, the Government declared its first industrial policy in April 1948, with a view to implement the recommendations of the Tripartite Industrial Conference and allaying the fears of the business community which had become panicky on the announcement of the report of the Economic Program Committee of the All India Congress Committee favouring nationalization of important industries and equal distribution of income. Thus on April 6, 1948, the country's national Government announced a very comprehensive policy with regards to where public sector and private sector co-exist. The Industrial Policy Resolution of 1948 envisaged that the "State must play a progressively active role in the development of industries". The industries were divided into 4 broad categories. They are -

1. *Exclusively State Monopoly:* The first category covered the manufacture of arms and ammunition, the production and control of atomic energy and the ownership and management of railway transport. The industries covered by the first category were to be the exclusive monopoly of the Central Government.

2. *Basic and Key industries:* The second category covered coal, iron and steel, aircraft manufacture, ship-building, manufacture of telephone, telegraphs and wireless apparatus excluding radio receiving sets and mineral oils. In the industries covered by the second category all new factories were to be owned and run by the Government but existing ones would continue to be run by private companies.

3. *Private Industries Controlled and regulated by the Government:* The third category covers industries of basic and strategic importance including salt, automobiles, tractors, prime movers, electric engineering, heavy machinery, machine tools, heavy chemicals, fertilizers, electro-chemical industries, non-ferrous metals, rubber manufacturers, power and industrial alcohol, cotton and wollen textiles, cement, sugar, paper and newsprint, and sea transport, minerals and industries relating to defence. In the industries covered by the third category, the central government would feel it necessary to plan and regulate them. It was emphasized that the central government could take over any industry vital for national defence. Thus, industries coming under this category belong to private enterprise but subject to state control.

4. *Completely Private Sector Industries:* The fourth category, comprising the "reminder of the industrial field". The residual of industrial field was left open to the private enterprises under the general control of the state.

It can be seen from the above paragraphs that the sphere of industries according to the Industrial Policy Resolution 1948 consists of two main parts, one reserved for the Government and the other left to private entrepreneurs. These two spheres are commonly called public sector and private sector. The most important feature, therefore, of the industrial policy resolution is that it established a "mixed economy" for our Country.

The Role of Small-Scale and Cottage Industries: The Industrial Policy Resolutions 1949 (IPR 48) emphasized the importance of cottage and small-scale industries in the economy. It was stressed that these industries offered scope for individual, village and co-operative enterprises. The IPR 48, gave due recognition to the importance of small-scale and cottage industries in the economy of India. It was visualized that they would be organized on co-operative lines and would be integrated and coordinated with large industries.

Steps towards better Industrial Relations: In keeping with the recommendations of the Industrial Conference of 1948, the Industrial Policy Resolution 1948, accepted profit-sharing and other schemes meant to associate labour with the management of industry as steps in the direction of more cordial Industrial Relations in the country.

Policy regulating Foreign Capital: The policy of regulating foreign capital was also clarified. The government recognized the need for securing the participation of foreign capital and enterprise particularly as regards industrial technique and knowledge so as to foster the pace of industrial technique and knowledge so as to foster the pace of industrialization of the Indian economy. But, the major interest in the ownership and control was to be in Indian hands, though it may be so in exceptional cases. To quote the Report of the Fiscal Commission (1949-50) —that as a rule, the major interest in ownership, an effective control, should always be in Indian hands. In all cases, however, the training of suitable Indian personnel for the purpose of eventually replacing foreign experts will be insisted upon". Thus, the government insisted upon the progressive Indianisation of foreign concerns.

The IPR 1948 laid the foundation for increasing participation of the state in the industrial activity. The respective roles of the public and private sector were clarified beyond any doubt. Thus, the IPR 1948 laid the foundation of a mixed economy in which both private and public sector would march together towards the goal of rapid industrial development.

Defects of IPR 1948: The major defects of the IPR 48 are enumerated below:

1. The State undertook the responsibility for large part of the country's industrial development, but it did not have technical and managerial manpower, necessary resources, finance etc., to undertake industrial development on a large scale.
2. The lack of co-ordination between the Union Government and State Government, poor experience, lack of technical know how, lack of adequate integration between policy and procedure in public sector etc., resulted in slow development of industries.
3. The most important drawback is the limit of 10 years prescribed by the Government to nationalize private industry. This created a doubt and suspicion in the minds of private entrepreneurs and retarded the growth of the private sector.
4. The evils of nepotism, favouritism, red-tapism percolated to all sphere of industries of the state.
5. It was criticized that Mixed Economy instead of taking

the merits of socialism and capitalism exhibited the evils of both the systems.

Thus, instead of laying a firm foundation of a mixed economy the IPR 1948 actually has ended up as a "mixed-up economy".

INDUSTRIAL POLICY RESOLUTION 1956

Since the declaration of industrial policy resolution 1948, several economic and political developments had occurred. Planning had proceeded on an organized basis. The first five-year plan was completed. At its 60th annual section the Indian National Congress adopted a resolution by which it committed itself to the establishment of a socialistic pattern of society in the country. Above all, the Parliament had accepted "the socialist pattern of society" as the basic aim of social and economic policy. Further the Government pledged itself to a large-scale program of industrial development. The target of investment in heavy industries and mining fixed at Rs.890 crores under the second five-year plan could be achieved only through a complete re-orientation of the industrial policy. These changes made it necessary to formulate a fresh industrial policy. It was in this context that the Government chose to re-state its industrial policy on 30th April 1956.

Objectives of IPR 1956: The industrial policy statement of 1956 was issued to achieve the following important objectives. They are -

1. To speed up industrialization and achieve a faster rate of economic growth.
2. To develop machine making and heavy industries.
3. To build up a large and growing co-operative sector.
4. To expand the public sector and

5. To reduce disparities in income and wealth and curb private monopolies.

Main Features of IPR 1956: The industrial policy was restated on April 30, 1956. The following were the important provision of the Industrial Policy Resolution 1956.

1. *New Classification of Industries:* The resolution, classified the industries under three heads namely Schedule A, Schedule B, and Schedule C.

Schedule A: - Seventeen industries were placed in Schedule A. They include arms and ammunition, atomic energy, iron and steel, heavy castings and forgings of iron and steel, heavy machinery required for iron and steel production, for mining, for machine tool manufacturers etc., heavy electrical industries; coal; mineral oils, mining, iron ore and other important minerals like copper, lead and zinc; aircraft; air transport, railway transport, shipbuilding; telephone, telegraph and wireless equipment; generation and distribution of electricity. The future development of these 17 industries was to be the exclusive responsibility of the state. All industries of basic and strategic importance or in the nature of public utility services were put in the public sector.

Schedule B: Twelve industries were placed in Schedule B. These 12 industries include other mining industries, aluminum and non-ferrous metals not included in Schedule A; machine tools, ferro-alloys and tool steels, the chemical industries; antibiotics and other essential drugs; fertilizers; synthetic rubber, carbonization of coal; chemical pulp; road transport and sea transport. These industries were to be progressively state owned. New undertakings under this category will be established in the public sector. But private enterprise will also be expected to supplement the efforts of the state. The private enterprise will also have opportunity to develop in this field either on its own or with state participation.

Schedule C: The remaining industries fall under Schedule C. They consisted of all those industries that do not come either under schedule A or schedule B. The development of these industries will be left to the initiative and enterprise of the private sector. The state will endeavour to facilitate and encourage the development of these industries in the private sector. For this purpose, the state will ensure to develop the transport system, power and other requirements for the development of the private sector. The state will also provide financial assistance to these industries.

It must be noted here that the above deviation of industries into separate categories is absolute. In other words, they are not being placed in watertight classification. The State may permit, in appropriate cases, privately owned units in industries falling within schedule A. Likewise, the State may start any industry even those falling in schedule C when the needs of planning require or there are other important considerations.

2. *Fair and Non-Discriminatory treatment for the Private Sector:* In order to induct confidence into the private sector, the Industrial Policy 1956, included many incentives and encouragements for the private sector. The State would continue to foster institutions to provide financial aid to private industries and special assistance would be given to enterprises organized on co-operative lines. The State would also endeavour to develop transport, power and other services. Further more, when there exist in the same industry both private and public owned industries; the policy of the state would be to give full and non-discriminatory treatment to both of them. Thus, the Government would continue to give all the benefits to private units that are being enjoyed by the public enterprises.

3. *Aid to Cottage and Small -Scale Industries:* The state would continue to follow the policy of supporting cottage

and small-scale Industries. This would be done either by restricting volume of production in the large-scale sector or by differentiate taxation or by direct subsidies. To increase the competitive strength of small-scale industries the state would take measures to improve and modernize the techniques of production. The aim of the state policy would be self-supporting and the development of cottage and small-scale Industries was to be integrated with the large-scale industry. For this purpose, the state would establish industrial estates, and rural community workshops, extension of rural electrification and the supply of power at cheap rates to help small-scale and cottage industries.

4. *Removal of Regional Imbalances:* The Resolution stressed the necessity of reducing the regional disparities in levels of development in order that industrialization may benefit the country as a whole. For this purpose, transport facilities, power supply and other facilities will be made available to areas which are at present lagging behind industrially and where there is greater need for providing opportunities for employment provided the location is otherwise suitable. The resolution fully supported the idea that only by securing a balanced and coordinated development of the industrial and the agricultural economy in each region can the entire country attain higher standards of living.

5. *Attitude towards foreign Capital*: The importance of foreign capital in our economic development was also duly recognized by the IPR 1956. Foreign investors have been given clear assurance for the safety of their interest and facilities for investment. Thus, the Government's attitude was the same as was enunciated in the IPR 1948.

6. *The need for the provision of amenities for Labour*: The Resolution emphasized the necessity of providing amenities and incentives for all those engaged in industry. It also stressed

the living and working conditions of the workers should be improved. It was also stressed that the workers and technicians should be associated progressively with the management. To set an example in this regard, the enterprises in the public sector have to set an example in this regard. Thus, the Resolution recognized the fact that in a socialistic society, the employees must be paid their due share in the profits of an enterprise.

7. *Co-operative Principle:* The IPR 56 felt that the principle of co-operation should be applied whenever possible and the private sector should be developed along co-operative lines.

Superiority of IPR 1956

The IPR 56 is considered as an improvement on the IPR 48 because of the following reasons. They are -

1. IPR 56 gave a wider field to the public sector.
2. IPR 56 abandoned the program of overall nationalization of industries.
3. It envisaged more cordial relations and co-operation between the private sector and public sector.
4. The IPR 56 promises a fair and non-discriminatory treatment of the private sector.
5. The IPR 56, emphasis on the development of the co-operative sector.
6. The classification of industries is made more flexible as there is no watertight classification of industries.

Critical Appraisal of IPR 1956: The IPR 56 was described as the economic constitution of India. Its object was to develop a socialist pattern of economy and reiterated the faith in the virtues of a "mixed economy". While it clearly demarcated the areas of public and private sectors, it was at the same time sufficiently flexible to make the required adjustment and modifications in the national interest. The IPR 56 stated clearly modifications in the national interest. The IPR 56 stated clearly the inherent right of the state to acquire any industrial undertaking. It also doubted the ability of the private sector to bring about fast economic development by itself. Therefore, we can say that the policy was designed to enable the Government in due course to gain a dominant position in the industrial sector.

The IPR 56 also secured for the private sector a permanent place in the economy. The public sector was not developed as a rival to the private sector. The policy endeavoured to create a congenial conditions and an infrastructure which would facilitate the growth of the private sector.

Therefore, the IPR 56 combined the above factors and the socialist orientation of the economic policy which gave the public sector such a predominant position which resulted in rapid expansion of the public sector. The private sector investment also increased in wake of public sector expansion. Thus, under the planned economy, the state had assumed the role of a senior partner to accelerate the pace of economic development.

INDUSTRIAL POLICY STATEMENT, 1977

In March 1977, the Congress Party for the first time in the history of free India was defeated in the general election. This paved the way for the Janata Party to assume power at the center. It made an industrial policy statement directed towards removing the distortions of the past so that the genuine aspirations of the people can be met within a time bound program of economic development". The policy statement mentioned that for the past 20 years, industry was governed by the IPR 56 which resulted in certain distortions like Unemployment has increased, rural-urban disparities have widened and the rate of real investment has stagnated. The growth of industrial output has been no more than three to four per cent per annum on the average. The incidence of industrial sickness has become widespread and some of the major industries are worst affected".

Thus, the Industrial Policy 1956, despite some desirable elements has resulted in certain limitations: -

(i) Unemployment has increased, rural-urban disparities have widened and the rate of real investment has stagnated. The growth of industrial output has been a mere 3% to 4% on the average.

(ii) The incidence of industrial sickness has become wide spread and some of the major industries are worst affected.

(iii) Only lip service was paid to the significant role-played by the small-scale and cottage industries, but in practice, it was the large-scale industries which were actively encouraged.

(iv) The large industrial houses were permitted to amass huge fortunes and diversify into various industries simply through borrowing funds from public sector financial institutions.

(v) A number of international giants had entered the country to take advantage of the sheltered and protected market in India but their role and position had not been clearly defined.

Therefore, the IPR 77 aimed at setting right the industrial economy of the country with the new resolution. The main thrust of the Janata Party's IPR 77 was to encourage small-scale and cottage industries as against the large-scale industries dominated by the big industrial houses. Encouragement of small-scale industries would lead to extension of employment and to reduce concentration of economic power.

However, the new policy was not in any way significantly different from the previous policy. The main elements of the new policy were:

1. Development of Small-Scale Sector: The main thrust of the IPR 77 was on effective promotion of cottage and small scale industries widely dispersed in rural areas and small towns. The policy stressed that "whatever can be produced by small and cottage industries must only be so produced". The list of industries that were excessively reserved for the small-scale sector was significantly expanded. The small-scale sector was classified into three categories:

(a) *Cottage and household industries* - includes industries which provide self-employment.

(b) *Tiny Sector* - includes industries in which investment is upto Rs. 1 lakh and situated in towns whose population is less than 50,000.

(c) *Small-scale industries* - includes industries in which investment is upto Rs. 10 lakhs and if there is ancillaries the investment will be raised up to Rs.15 lakhs.

The IPR 77 intends to develop the above-mentioned categories of Industry. The measures suggested for their promotion include the following: -

1. Under IPR 56, 180 items were reserved for small-scale industries. This list was expanded to 807 items under IPR 77.

2. For the development of small scale and cottage industries, the policy proposed to set up "District Industries Center" (DIC) in each district. The DIC would provide the support required by small scale and cottage industries. This agency would provide all the financial and managerial assistance to the small-scale industries under a single roof.

3. The IPR 77, proposed to create special programs for the development of Khadi and Village industries.
4. A separate wing of the IDBI would exclusively deal with the credit requirements of small, village and cottage industries.
5. Special arrangements were to be made to provide suitable technology for small and village industries with a view to improve their productivity and also for increasing the earning capacity of the workers in such industries.

2. *Area for Large-Scale Industries:* - The IPR 77 prescribed the following areas for the Large-Scale sector. They are -

(a) Basic industries like steel, nonferrous metals, cement, oil refineries etc., which provide infrastructure for the small-scale and village industries.

(b) Capital goods industries needed for meeting the machinery requirements of small-scale and basic industries.

(c) High technology industries like fertilizers, pesticides, and petrochemicals etc., which require large scale production and whose products are used by agriculture and small-scale industries.

(d) Other industries which were outside the list of items reserved for small-scale industries.

3. *Approach towards Large Business Houses:* To ensure that large business houses do not acquire a dominant or monopolistic position in the market, it was suggested that large business houses would have to rely on their own resources for financing new projects or expansion of the existing ones. The IPR 77 wanted to implement the provisions of the M.R.T.P. Act vigorously to curb the growing concentration of economic power.

4. *Expanding Role for Public-Sector:* The IPR 77 specified that the public sector besides producing strategic goods of basic nature, would also be responsible for encouraging the development of a wide range of ancillary industries and making available its expertise in technology and management to small-scale and cottage industry.

5. *Approach towards Foreign Collaboration:* As a rule, the majority interest in ownership and control should be in Indian hands. Though in exceptional cases, the Government may ignore this rule. In areas where foreign technological know-how is not needed, existing collaborations will not be renewed and such foreign companies must change their priorities within the framework of the Foreign Exchange Regulation Act (FERA).

6. *Promotion of Technological Self-Reliance*: In areas where Indian skills and technology were not adequately developed, the Government permitted the inflow of technology. This was done in high priority areas in order to promote technological self-reliance. The Governments preference would be for outright purchase of the best available technology and than adopting such technology to the country's needs.

7. *Approach towards Sick Units:* The policy stated that unless in cases which involve the loss of employment for many and the commitment of huge public funds, the sick units will not be generally taken over.

8. *Management-Labour Relations:* There was considerable loss of industrial production owing to labour unrest particularly after the lifting of the Emergency. The Government decided to examine the possibilities of encouraging worker's participation in the equity of industrial units without in any way, adversely affecting their interests. Such equity participation together with an active association of workers in decision-making from the shop floor level to the board

level would provide necessary environment for a meaningful participation by workers in the management of industry.

CRITICAL EVALUATION OF INDUSTRIAL POLICY 1977

The main threat of the IPR 77 was to encourage small scale and cottage industries as against the large-scale industries dominated by big industrial houses and multi-nationals. It was also suggested that such an encouragement of the small industries would on the one hand lead to extension of employment and on the other lead to a reduction in concentration of economic power.

The basic thrust of the Policy was the promotion of small-scale industries. Among the measures listed for their promotion are: -

- Reservation or demarcation of spheres of production.
- Non-Expansion of the capacity of large-scale industry and

  Imposition of a cess on large-scale industry.

All the above-mentioned measures that the IPR 77 listed were there in the IPR 56. All that the IPR 77 did was to expand the list of 180 items reserved for the small scale industries were increased to 807 items. Contrary to common belief, the IPR 77 did not contain any radical policies regarding multinationals but continued the policy which was followed since 1948. In fact, the foreign companies and multinationals that were prepared to follow the existing rules and regulations were welcome. However, they were asked to reduce their share of equity under the FERA. But in the case of sophisticated technologies, they were even permitted to have cent percent equity.

INDUSTRIAL POLICY 1980

The fall of the Janatha Party Government at the center eventually brought fresh parliamentary election. The parliamentary election brought the Congress (I), led by Mrs. Indira Gandhi, back to power with a thumping majority. The new Government announced its Industrial Policy on 23rd July 1980. Outlining the philosophy behind the IPR 1980, the minister for Industries stated: -"The Industrial Policy announcement of 1956 in fact reflects the value system of our country and has shown conclusively the merit of constructive flexibility. In terms of this resolution, the task of raising the pillars of economic infrastructure in the country was entrusted to the public sector for reasons of its greater reliability, for the very large investments required and the longer gestation periods of the projects crucial for economic development. The 1956 resolution, therefore, forms the basis of this statement". The IPR 80 aimed at optimum utilization of installed capacity, maximization of productivity, strengthening of agricultural base and removal of regional imbalances. The IPR 80 was based on the IPR 56.

Socio-economic objectives: The socio-economic objectives of the IPR 80 were set out as under.

1. Optimum utilization of the installed capacities in various industries.
2. Maximizing production and achieving higher productivity.
3. Higher employment generation.
4. Correction of regional imbalance through a preferential development of industrially backward areas.
5. Strengthening of the agricultural base by according a preferential treatment of agro-based industries, and promoting optimum inter-sectoral relationship.

6. Faster promotion of export oriented and import substitution industries.
7. Promoting economic federalism with an equitable spread of investment and the dispersal of returns among widely spread over small but growing units in rural as well as urban areas.
8. To revive the economy which is inhibited by infrastructural gaps and inadequacies in performance, the following policy measures were proposed.
   - Effective operational management of the public sector.
   - Integrating industrial development in private sector by promoting the concept of economic federalism.
   - Promotion of industries in rural. areas.
   - Regularisation of unauthorized excess capacity installed in the private sector.
   - Management of sick units would be taken over only on grounds of public interest.

Features of IPR 80: - The main features of the IPR 80 are as follows: -

1. The revival of the economic structure.
2. Revitalizing the public sector.
3. Dynamic role of the private sector.
4. Establishment of economic federalism.
5. Setting up nucleus plants.
6. Encouragement and support to small-scale and village industries by redefining small units, financial support, building up buffer stocks of critical inputs, giving marketing support and reservation of items.

7. Removing regional imbalances.
8. Generating of employment of higher production.
9. Liberalization of existing capacities.
10. Streamlining of licensing procedures.
11. Encouraging export-oriented units,
12. Provision for research and development.
13. Transfer of technology.
14. Modernization packages and energy industry dovetailing.
15. Setting up monitoring system and data bank.
16. Evaluation of industries.
17. Tackling industrial sickness through mergers or amalgamation.
18. Improving industrial relations and
19. Adopting appropriate industrial pricing policy.

Some of the important features are discussed below.

Revitalization the Public Sector: The Industrial Policy stressed that the public sector should became the peoples sector rather than a no body's sector. It has to be recast in its role, management and strategy. For this purpose, the policy stated that a time bound program should be chalked out for revitalization of the public sector. Under such a program measures will be taken for improvement of the various functional fields such as marketing, financing, communication system etc.

Re-definition of small units: The IPR 80 has redefined the small units to ensure their faster growth. The investment limits for small units are given below.

(a) To increase the limit of investment in the case of tiny units from Rs. 1 lakh to Rs. 2 lakh.

(b) To increase the unit of investment in case of small scale units from Rs. 10 lakhs to Rs. 20 lakhs; and

(c) To increase the limit of investment in the case of ancillaries from Rs. 15 lakhs to Rs. 25 lakhs.

The Government decided to increase the investment limits in order to boost the development of small-scale industries.

Setting up nucleus plants: While making all efforts towards integrated industrial development, the IPR 80, proposed to promote the concept of economic federalism with setting up of a few nucleus plants in each district, identified as industrially backward, to generate as many ancillaries and small and cottage units as possible.

Removal of regional imbalances: It was stated in the policy statement that industrialization would be geared to correct the regional imbalances. The policy calls upon emergence of a network ancillaries spread out in backward areas linked with the local resources and talents. Public and private sectors should both join in the removal of regional imbalances through dispersal of industrialization.

Provision for automatic growth: Automatic expansion of large scale industries is a important concession given in the IPR 80. This facility of automatic expansion to is provided all industries specified in the first schedule of the Industrial Development and Regulation Act 1951.

Provision for Research and Development: The IPR 80 suggested the extension of concession in respect of imports and other benefits for the industries which intend to strengthen research and development. The concept of district industries centre has been abandoned and idea of nucleus plants in each district is sort to be introduced for ancillary industries in the rural sector.

Provision for sick units: Sick units would be taken over only when it is absolutely necessary in the public interest. Units guilty of mis-management would be firmly dealt with. The Government would think liberalizing tax concessions to bring about amalgamation of sick units with healthy units on the basis of potential viability.

Assessment of New Industrial Policy 1980

The IPR80 endorsed the view of the IPR 56. The Industrial Policy 1980 intended to follow a "pragmatic" approach. The implications of the IPR 80 are as follows: -

1. The IPR 80 accepted that there has been an erosion of faith in public sector in recent years. Therefore, the government decided to launch a drive to revive the efficiency of public sector undertakings.
2. To promote the growth of small-scale industries, the IPR 80, proposed to increase the investment limits for small-scale sector, from Rs.10 lakhs to Rs. 20 lakhs. The investment limits for ancillary units is proposed to be increased from the existing Rs. 15 lakhs to Rs. 25 lakhs.
3. The IPR 80 emphasized the need to promote suitable industries in rural areas to generate higher employment and higher income for the villagers.
4. To remove regional imbalances, the IPR 80 decided to encourage the dispersal of industry and setting up of units in industrially backward areas.
5. The IPR 80 introduced "a checklist to serve as *'early warning system'* for identifying symptoms of sickness" in industries. With regard to industrial sickness, the statement also emphasized that it would encourage merger of sick units with healthy units which are capable of managing the sick units.

7. The IPR 80 provided ample scope for the private sector to expand its activities and even set up industries in the sector reserved for the state in the IPR 56.

The Industrial Policy 1980 was guided merely by considerations of growth. The distinction between large-scale industries and small-scale industries was blurred. This helped the big businesses at the cost of small-scale industries. Thus we can say that the IPR 80 chose a more capital-intensive path of development and underplayed the employment objectives.

INDUSTRIAL POLICY RESOLUTION 1985

The committee appointed by Government in January 1984, to examine the principles of a possible shift from physical to financial controls submitted its report in January 1985. In pursuance of the recommendations and findings of the committee, a major policy statement was made in December 1985 to further liberalize industrial policy and procedures.

Objectives of IPR 85: The main objectives of the IPR 85 are given below: -

1. Accelerate industrial growth by increasing production.
2. Maximize capacity utilization and
3. Encourage setting up of industrial units in listed backward regions.

Salient Features of IPR 85: The salient features of IPR 85 are given below.

1. Setting up Industrial units in backward areas.
2. The export obligation has been reduced to 25% for category 'B' and 'C' districts. The stipulation would be dispensed with for category 'A' districts. The objective of reduction in export obligation was to industrializing backward areas in the country.

3. The limit of foreign exchange requirement for import of raw materials and components was raised to Rs. 75 lakhs subject to a ceiling of 15% of the ex-factory value of the annual production.
4. The IRP 85 has permitted more items which can be taken up for production by large business houses and MRTP and FERA companies.
5. A simplified procedure will be followed for modernization, replacement or renovation, if it results in an increase in the capacity up to 49% of the licensed capacity.
6. The facility of getting the industrial licenses re-endorsed will be available to all licensed units which have achieved 80% of their licensed capacity during any of the preceding five years preceding 31 March 1985.
7. The delicensing scheme will be extended to MRTP Act.

Assessment of IPR 85: The IPR 85 represented a departure from the past policies in its greater reliance on the private sector and on modern technology. The measures of liberalization of licensing following on the earlier delicensing of a number of industries were bound to encourage investment and increase production. This will promote industrial growth. Therefore, the measures indicated in the IPR 85 were steps in the right direction.

INDUSTRIAL POLICY 1990

The Janata Dal Government announced its Policy Resolution on 31st May 1990.

The Objectives of IPR 90: - The IPR 90 has been designed to achieve the following objectives:

(a) Employment generation at a fast pace.

(b) Dispersal of industry in the rural areas; and

(c) To enhance the contribution of small-scale industries to exports.

Features of IPR 90: The IPR 90 seeks to reorient industrial growth. The Industrial Policy made a case for the growth of the small-scale industries just on the lines of the IPR 77. The salient features of IPR 90 are given below.

1. The Promotion of Small-Scale Industries: The IPR 90, had as its objective to reorient industries to generate employment and to disperse industries to rural areas. Keeping this objective in mind, the IPR 90, has decided to take the following measures

(a) *Increase in investment ceiling*: The investment ceiling in plant and machinery for small-scale industries has been redefined. The ceiling fixed in 1985 at Rs. 35 lakhs was now raised to Rs. 60 lakhs. The investment ceiling for ancillary units that had a ceiling of Rs. 45 lakhs has been raised to 75 lakhs. The investment ceiling in respect of tiny units has been raised from the present Rs. 2 lakhs to Rs. 5 lakhs. However, with regard to their location, the population limit of 5000 as per 1981 census would continue to apply.

(b) *Reservation of Industries for the small-scale sector*: Presently, 836 items have been reserved exclusively for the small-scale sector. The medium and large-scale sector can enter this area only if they want to export. According to IPR 90, efforts would be made to identify more time amenable to similar reservation.

(c) *Modernization and up Gradation of Technology*: With a view to improving the competitiveness of the products manufactured in small scale sector, programs for modernization and up gradation of technology would be implemented. A number of technology centres, tool rooms, process and product development centres, testing centres, etc., will be set up under the umbrella of an apex technology development centre in Small Industries Development Organization.

(d) *Investment Subsidy*: A new scheme of central investment subsidy exclusively for the small scale sector in rural and backward areas capable of generating higher level of employment at lower capital cost would be implemented.

(e) *Credit for Small Scale Industries*: The major tasks of SIDBI, Commercial banks, and financial institutions would be to canalise need based higher flow of credit, both by way of term loan and working capital, to the tiny and rural industries. A new apex bank known as SIDBI has already been established to ensure adequate and timely flow of credit for the small-scale industries.

(f) *Reduction of Bureaucratic Control*: One of the persistent complaints of the small-scale units is their being subjected to a large number of laws. The IPR 90 seeks to reduce these bureaucratic controls so that unnecessary interference is eliminated.

2. Promotion of Agro-based Rural Industries: -

(a) *Creation of Specific Marketing Organization*: Special marketing organizations at the centre and state levels shall be created to assist rural artisans in marketing their products and also to supply the raw materials.

(b) *Provision of credit facilities*: Agro-processing industry would receive high priority in credit allocation from the financial institutions. Besides, providing concessional credit, training facilities and free consultancy to groups of artisans will also be provided.

(c) *Location of Agro-based Industries in Rural Areas:* In sectors, where units require licensing, the policy would also encourage location of processing units in rural areas where growers are concentrated. Apart from economic benefits of proximity to raw materials it would help in dispersal of industry and increasing employment in rural areas.

(d) *Promotion of Joint Ownership in Agro-processing Industries:* The success of agro-based industries is ensured through close links forged between growers and processors. The new industrial policy, therefore, seeks to promote projects which are organized on the basis of joint ownership. Growers will be encouraged to set up processing units within the institutional framework. This will also ensure the transmission of better technology for enhanced agricultural production.

3. *Delicensing of industries:* All new units up to an investment of Rs. 25 crores in fixed assets in non-backward areas and Rs. 75 crores in centrally notified backward areas will be exempted from requirement of obtaining license.

4. *Import of capital goods:* For the import of capital goods, the entrepreneur would have entitlement of import up to a landed value of 30% of the total value of plant and machinery required for the unit.

5. *Import of Raw Materials and Components:* - The imports of raw materials and components will be permissible up to a landed value of 30% of the ex-factory value of annual production. Raw materials and components eligible for import under open general license will not be included within this 30%.

6. *Broad Handling Scheme:* The existing broad-branding

scheme would continue to be in force. However, this would not include those items which are reserved for small scale sector.

7. Foreign Investment: In order to attract effective inflow of technology, investment upto 40% of equity will be allowed on an automatic basis. In such proposals, the landed value of imported capital goods shall not exceed 30% of the value of plant and machinery.

8. Foreign Collaboration: In respect of transfer of technology, if an entrepreneur considers necessary to import technology, he can conclude an agreement with the collaborator, without obtaining any clearance from the government provided that royalty payment does not exceed 5% on domestic sales and 8% on exports.

9. Export Oriented Units: 100% export oriented units (EOUs) and units to be set up in export processing zones (EPZs) are also being delicensed under the scheme up to an investment limit of Rs. 75 crores. Units set up by MRTP/FERA Companies will be covered by the procedures set out above, but they will continue to need clearances under the provisions and regulations of these two Acts.

An Evaluation of IPR 90: - The IPR 90 made a case for the growth of the small-scale industries just on the lines of the IPR 77. The Implications of the IPR 90 is as follows: -

1. The initiatives proposed in the IPR 90 is bound to increase the competitive strength of the small units by improving their quality of output and reducing their costs.
2. Efforts to eliminate bureaucratic interference so that the small-scale entrepreneurs are not harassed is a important plus point in the IPR 90.

3. The linking of growers with processing units and encouraging joint ownership of projects is a rationalization which is intended to provide a boost to agro-based units.
4. The IPR 90 intends to identify more items amenable to reservation besides the 836 items included in the list. But in all these items, big business and large sector dominate. Therefore, the enlargement of reservation list is not important but improving the market share of the small scale sector by phasing out the large scale sector from this area is necessary.
5. 100% export oriented units (EOUs) and units to be set up in export processing zones (EPZs) are also being delicensed under the scheme unto an investment of Rs. 75 crores. This again will open the import window further in the name of export promotion.
6. Though the IPR 90 by its entire policy of promotion of small scale and agro based industries aimed to increase the market share of the small sector in total industrial output, there is greater evidence of shrinkage in the market share of the small sector in view of the serious encroachments that the large sector has made recently.
7. The market mechanism is not the best allocator of resources in socially desirable channels. This fact seems to have conveniently escaped the attention of new policy framers. Total de-regulation is bound to usher in an era of distortions of industrial growth.
8. The IPR 90 allows established industries to claim import license for capital goods as well as raw materials and components with the balance of payments situation already very adverse, the IPR 90 will add to the burden of imports.

It is apt to conclude with the views of the Samajvadi Janta Party leader Chandra Shaker that "the new industrial policy (IPR 90) has opened the doors of the Indian economy to multinationals which might reduce the country to a banana republic. The new industrial policy has not dealt with any of the basic problems like industrial sickness, public sector maladies and non-essential consumer goods".

NEW INDUSTRIAL POLICY 1991

The IPR 56 gave primacy to the role of the state to assume a predominant and direct responsibility for industrial development. However, the IPR 85 and IPR 90 shifted the focus from controls to liberalization. The net result of all these changes got manifested in the form of acceleration in industrial growth rate and structural transformation in the industrial scenario. The New Industrial Policy 1991 aims at continuing the policy of liberalization to its logical end by completely unshackling the Indian industrial economy from unnecessary bureaucratic control.

The Objectives of IPR 1991: On 24th July 1991, the Congress (I) Government led by Mr. Narasimha Rao announced the new industrial policy 1991. The main objective of the new industrial policy is to introduce liberalization with a view to integrate the Indian economy with the world economy. Keeping this view in mind the restrictions on direct foreign investment was removed. The IPR 91 also freed the domestic entrepreneur from the restrictions of MRTP Act. The policy also aims to shed the load of the public enterprises.

The following are the main objectives of the IPR 91.

1. To attain technological dynamism and international competitiveness.
2. To build on the gains already made in the industrial sector.

3. To maintain a sustained growth in productivity and gainful employment and
4. To correct the distortions or weakness that may creep in the pattern of industrial growth.

The Main Features of the Industrial Policy Statement 1991: In order to achieve the objectives mentioned above, the Government tabled the Industrial Policy Statement on 24 the July 1991 in the Lok Sabha. It contained a series of initiatives in respect of policies in the following areas: -

(1) Industrial licensing policy.
(2) Foreign investment policy.
(3) Foreign technology policy.
(4) Public sector policy.
(5) MRTP Act.

The salient features of the policy are discussed below: -

Industrial Licensing Policy: The new industrial policy statement has put accent upon the need for a continuation of liberalized industrial licensing, procedures and approvals for a full realization of the industrial potential of the country. This calls for bold and imaginative decisions designed to remove restraints on capacity creation, which at the same time, ensure that over-riding national interests are not sacrificed. Thus, in the sphere of industrial licensing, the role of the government was to be changed from that of only exercising control to one of providing help and guidance by making essential procedures fully transparent and by eliminating delays. Keeping the above-mentioned principles in mind the following decisions have been taken.

(a) *Delicensing:* The industrial licensing will be abolished for all projects except for those which are important for security, strategic, social and environmental reasons. The compulsory licensing provisions would apply only to industries such as coal and lignite, petroleum, distillation and brewing of alcoholic drink, sugar, cigars and cigarettes, motor cars, plywood, industrial explosives, hazardous chemicals, drugs and pharmaceuticals, entertainment electronic, paper and newsprint, animal fats and oils, air-conditioners, refrigerators, microwave ovens and domestic washing machines. However, compulsory licensing will not apply for small-scale sector and existing units exempted from industrial licensing.

(b) *Reservation for Public Sector:* Industries such as arms and ammunition and allied items of defence equipment, atomic energy, mineral oils, mining of iron ore, manganese ore, chrome ore, sulphur, gypsum, gold and diamond, mining of copper, tin, lead and zinc and railway transport are reserved for the public sector.

(c) *Automatic clearance of Imports of Capital Goods:* The IPR 91 seeks to give automatic clearance for the imports of capital goods subject to the availability of foreign exchange. Therefore in cases where foreign exchange availability is ensured through foreign equity if the CIF value of imported capital goods required is less than 25% of total value of plant and equipment, up to a maximum value of Rs. 2 crores, Automatic clearance will be given.

(d) *Location Policy:* If industries are located in cities where the population is less than one million, there will be no need to obtain industrial approval from the Central Government. However, land use regulation and environmental legislation will continue to regulate industrial locations.

(e) *Abolition of Registration Schemes:* All existing registration schemes will be abolished. The owners of Industries will only be required to file an information memorandum on new projects and substantial expansions.

Foreign Investment Policy: The IPR 91 has recognized the fact that Indian industry can scarcely be competitive with the rest of the world if the acquisition of technological capability is subject to regulatory environment. Therefore, in order to invite foreign investment in high priority industries, requiring large investments and advanced technology, it has been decided to provide approval for direct foreign investment upto 51% foreign equity in such industries. The following policy measures have been announced. They are -

(a) *Automatic Approval for Technology Agreements in High Priority Industries:* The IPR 91 accords automatic approval for foreign technology agreements in high priority industries up to a lump sum payment of Rs. 1 crore, 5% royalty for domestic sales, and 8% for exports, subject to total payments of 8% of sales over 10 year period from the date of agreement or 7 years from commencement of production.

(b) *Automatic Approval for Technology Agreements in Industries other than High Priority Industries:* The IPR 91 has created provision for automatic approval for technology agreements in industries other than high priority industries, provided no free foreign exchange is required for any payments.

(c) *Services of Foreign Technicians:* According to IPR 91, no permission is necessary to hire foreign technicians. However, payments may be made from blanket permits or free foreign exchange according to Reserve Bank of India's guidelines.

Public Sector Policy: Public enterprises have shown a very low rate of return on the capital invested. The result is that many of the public enterprises have become a burden rather than being an asset to the Government. The IPR 91 has emphasized the need for a new approach to public enterprises. Accordingly, measures must be taken to make these enterprises more growth oriented and technically dynamic. The following policy measures have been announced.

(a) *Review of Portfolio of Public Sector Investment:* Portfolio of public sector investment will be reviewed with a view to focus the public sector on strategic, high-tech and essential infrastructure. Whereas some reservation for the public sector is being retained there would be no bar for areas exclusively to be opened up to the private selectively. Similarly the public sector will also be allowed entry in areas not reserved for it.

(b) *Rehabilitation Schemes for Sick Public Enterprises:* Public enterprises which are chronically sick and which are unlikely to be turned around will be referred to the Board for Industrial and Financial Reconstruction (BIFR) or other similar high level institutions created for this purpose. A social security mechanism will be created to protect the interests of workers likely to be affected by such rehabilitation packages.

(c) *Resource Mobilization and Public Participation:* In order to raise resources and encourage wider public participation, a part of the Government's shareholdings in the public sector would be offered to mutual funds, financial institutions, general public and workers.

(d) *Professionalisation of Management:* Boards of public sector companies would be made more professional and given greater powers.

(e) *Thrust on Performance Improvement:* There will be a greater thrust on performance improvement through the memorandum of understanding (MOU) system through which managements would be granted greater autonomy and will be held accountable.

Therefore, it is time the Government adopts a new approach to public enterprises units which may be faltering at present but are potentially viable must be restructured and given a new lease of life.

The priority areas for growth of public enterprises in future will be as follows:

(a) Essential infrastructure goods and services.

(b) Exploration and exploitation of oil and mineral resources.

(c) Technology development and building of manufacturing capabilities in areas which are crucial in the long-term development of the economy and where private sector investment is inadequate.

(d) Manufacture of products where strategic considerations predominate such defence equipment.

The Government should strengthen those public enterprises which fall in the reserved areas of operation. Such enterprises should be provided a much greater degree of management autonomy. Competition should also be induced by inviting private sector participation. In the case of selected enterprises, part of Government holdings in the equity share capital of these enterprises should be disinvested in order to provide further market discipline to the performance of public enterprises.

Monopolies and Restrictive Trade Practices Act (MRTP): The interference of the Government through the MRTP Act in investment decisions of large companies has become deleterious in its effects on Indian industrial growth.

The IPR 91, thus seeks to amend the MRTP Act to remove the threshold limits of assets in respect of MRTP companies and dominant undertakings. Thus, the thrust of the MRTP Act will be more on controlling unfair or restrictive business practices rather than making it necessary for the monopoly houses to obtain prior approval of central government for expansion, establishment of new undertakings and appointment of certain directors. The following are the changes to be made in the MRTP Act -

(a) The MRTP Act will be emended to remove the threshold limits of assets in respect of MRTP companies and dominant undertakings. This eliminates the requirement of prior approval of Central Government for establishment of new undertakings, expansion of undertakings, merger, amalgamation and takeovers appointment of Director under certain circumstances.

(b) Emphasis will be placed on controlling and regulating monopolistic, restrictive and unfair trade practices. Simultaneously, the newly empowered MRTP Commission will be authorised to initiate investigations suo moto or on complaints received from individual consumers or classes of consumers in regard to monopolistic, restrictive and unfair trade practices.

An Evaluation of IPR 91: In view of the considerations outlined above, the Government has decided to take a series of measures to unshackle the Indian industrial economy from the unnecessary bureaucratic control. These measures complement the other series of measures being taken by Government in these areas of trade policy, exchange rate management, fiscal policy, financial sector reform and overall macro-economic management. The IPR 91 can be regarded as a realistic economic constitution governing the growth of industrial sector. It is based on the thesis of liberal economic order. It will certainly give an impetus to the inflow of foreign investment and technological up gradation in Indian industries.

It is expected to act as an instrument to promote optimal size and pattern of industrial growth.

All these provisions have been welcomed by the business circles. There is an overall relief in the dismantling of industrial licensing and regime of control.

However, there are several other areas which have been criticized. They are -

(i) The IPR 91 has decided to approve up to 51% foreign equity in high priority industries. Further, the Government will also permit 100% foreign equity if the entire output is exported. The free flow of foreign capital will be detrimental to self-reliance.

(ii) The idea of free flow of foreign capital is being done to provide the much needed foreign exchange. However, in our over enthusiasm to welcome foreign capital, the fear is that we may sell our sovereignty to multinationals.

(iii) Another criticism is that, once foreign capital is permitted free entry, the distinction between high priority and low priority industries will gradually disappear over time and all lines of production will be opened to facilitate foreign investment.

(iv) Foreign capitalists, after establishing their corporations in the country, shall ask for remittance of profits and dividends and royalties. With foreign debt burden already becoming heavy, prudence demands that utmost care can be taken to invite foreign capital in high priority industries only, otherwise the country may suffer by following the path of Brazil or Mexico.

(v) The IPR 91 has attempted to evade the question on social security mechanism. The IPR 91 only intends to refer the cases of sick industries to the BIFR. Thus, the Industrial Policy statement has only sidetracks the issues and has generated a fear in the mind of the workers that the Government is not sincere in protecting the interest of the workers.

(vi) The IPR 91 has restricted the work of MRTP Commission to controlling and regulating monopolistic, restrictive and unfair trade practices. This will certainly work against the interest of the small and medium scale industries, as big business will systematically eliminate them.

QUESTIONS
(for Self-Study)

1. Industrial policy resolution 1956 is regarded as the economic constitution of India. How far do you agree with this view?
2. Write a brief note on Industrial policy statement 1980.
3. Discuss the features of Industrial Policy Resolution of 1948.
4. Discuss the policy pursued by the Government of India towards the development of Industries.

UNIVERSITY QUESTIONS

(15 Marks)

- Explain the main contents of industrial policy statement 1980 (October/November 2004)
- Explain the main contents of the Industrial Policy Resolution 1956. (April 2004)
- Give the main features of Industrial Policy 1980 (April/May 2003)
- What are the Socio-Economic objectives of the Industrial policy 1980? (April/May 2003)
- Narrate in brief the main contents of the new Industrial Policy 1991? (October 2002)
- Narrate the main contents of the New Industrial Policy 1991.(April/May1997)

(5 Marks)

- Give a brief note on the features of industrial policy 1956. (October 1996)
- Mention the findings of the Hazari Committee report. (October 1996)

(1Mark)

- Give the structure of industries according to IPR 1956. .(April/ May1997)

6

INDUSTRIAL LICENSING POLICIES

Learning Objectives

After going through this chapter, you will be conversant with:

- Objectives of Industrial Licensing
- Considerations governing the grant of Industrial Licenses
- Industrial (Development and Regulation) Act, 1951
- Industrial Licensing in India
- New Licensing Policy and Process 1970
- Licensing Policy of 1973
- Licensing Policy of 1975
- Licensing Policy of 1980
- Licensing Policy of 1982
- Liberalization measures of 85 and 86
- Licensing Policy of 1988
- Licensing Policy of 1991

An under developed country like India, seeking rapid economic development, suffers from certain serious resource shortage like shortage of capital, shortage of technology, shortage of foreign exchange etc. It also suffers from economic inequalities and concentration of economic power in the hands of monopoly houses and dominant undertakings. Further more; the Indian economy also suffers from certain imbalances and inequalities like regional imbalance between agricultural sector and industrial sector etc. In order to set right these anomalies industrial license is necessary. It is the purpose of industrial licensing to make an optimum use of the scarce resources, redress the various imbalances and reduce inequalities as far as possible. The term license refers to a written permission from the Government to an industrial undertaking to manufacture specific articles included in the schedule. It includes particulars of the industrial undertakings, its location, the articles to be manufactured, details of capacity and other appropriate conditions which are enforceable under the law. Licensing is a means to help achieve some of the objectives of industrial policy. The system of industrial licensing was introduced in India to give effect to the IPR 48. Since then it has continued to operate and from time to time some modifications have been introduced.

OBJECTIVES OF INDUSTRIAL LICENSING

The main objectives of licensing policy are: -

1. To develop and regulate industrial investment and production according to priorities and targets of various plans.
2. To protect and to encourage small and medium entrepreneurs.
3. To prevent concentration of economic power in the hands of a few individuals or a group of individuals.
4. To balance economic development of different regions and to reduce disparities in the levels of industrial development.
5. To make an optimum use of the limited capital resources so that they are invested in vital industries and not frittered away on unnecessary or less important industries.
6. To promote and develop small and village industries.

7. To promote export-oriented industries so that the country could earn valuable foreign exchange.
8. To build up a self-reliant economy.
9. To promote industries which are fuel efficient with the object to conserve energy.
10. To promote industries in areas which preserve ecological balance.
11. To develop a new class of enlightened entrepreneurs.

CONSIDERATIONS GOVERNING THE GRANT OF INDUSTRIAL LICENSE

In taking a decision on Industrial License applications, the following principles or considerations are kept in mind.

1. The policy frame work contained in the industrial policy resolution.
2. The detailed considerations set out in the Governments statement on the licensing policy.
3. The priorities and production targets of current five year plans and the annual plans.
4. The techno-economic considerations relevant to particular industry.
5. The techno-economic features of the project under consideration.

The following are the other important features with reference to which Industrial license applications are examined.

1. The priority of the industry as outlined in the plan.
2. Whether the proposed investment confirms to the policy outlined in the licensing policy statement.
3. The net effect on balance of payments taking into accounts the export possibilities and import savings.

4. Locational aspects in the light of removal of regional imbalances.
5. The extent to which the proposed project will be utilizing the indigenous know-how.
6. The direct and indirect employment potential.
7. Whether commercial production is proposed to be achieved in a realistic time period.
8. Whether the process proposed to be adopted is efficient from the techno-economic point of view.

Industrial licensing is an essential part of the industrial policy. It is an instrument for effective implementation of the industrial policy. It is through industrial licensing that the main objectives of Government's industrial policy have to be achieved.

INDUSTRIAL (DEVELOPMENT AND REGULATION) ACT 1951

The Industrial Development and Regulation Act was passed in 1951. The act aims at enabling the Government to secure the objectives of industrial policy such as regulating industrial development, avoidance of monopoly, protection of small-scale industries etc. To achieve these objectives, the Government should have the power to direct, regulate and control factors like industrial investment, location, expansion and growth, management etc. The Industrial development and regulation Act 1951, amended from time to time is the most effective weapon the Government possesses in its armoury. The Act also confers on the Government the power to make rules for regulating the production and development of Industries in the Schedule.

The Act extends to the whole of India (including Jammu and Kashmir). Its provisions apply to all "industrial undertakings" manufacturing any of the items included in the First Schedule of the act. The Act defines "an industrial undertaking as any undertaking pertaining to a scheduled industry carried on in one or more factories".

A 'factory' means "any premises including the precincts thereof, in any part of which a manufacturing process is being carried on or is ordinarily so carried on:

(i) With the aid of power, provided that fifty or more workers are working or were working thereon on any day of the preceding twelve months.

(ii) Without the aid of power, provided that one hundred or more workers are working or were working thereon on any day of the preceding twelve months and provided further that in no part of such premises any manufacturing process is being carried on with the aid of power.

The Important Provisions of the IDR Act: The important provisions of the act were:

(i) No new industrial units could be established or substantial extension to existing plants made without a license from the Central Government and while granting license for new undertakings, Government could lay down conditions regarding location, minimum size etc., if necessary.

(ii) Government could make investigation into certain specified industries or undertakings in industries:

(a) Which showed a fall in production;

(b) Which showed deterioration in quality of the product;

(c) Which showed a rise in the price of the product;

(d) Which showed tendencies in the directions mentioned in (a) (b) and (c) above,

(e) Which used resources of national importance; and

(f) Which were managed in a manner likely to do harm to the interests of the shareholders or customers;

The Government could also issue proper directions for rectifying the above mentioned drawbacks.

(iii) Government could take under its own management undertakings which failed to carry out its instructions for improvement in management and policies.

(iv) The Government could prescribe prices, methods and the volume of production and channels of distribution.

(v) The Government is empowered by the Act to set up development councils for the individual or groups of industries.

The Central Advisory Council

The Central Advisory Council was established in May, 1952. Its main function was to advise Government concerning the development and regulation of the scheduled industries. The Advisory Council consists of a chairman and members not exceeding thirty. All are appointed by the Government. When the members of the council are picked representation is given to the various interest groups like owners, employees, consumers, primary suppliers etc., from the industrial undertakings in the scheduled industries.

Sec 5 of the IDR Act empowers the Central Government to establish a Central Advisory Council.

Development Councils

The Development Councils consisting of representatives of industry, labour, management and consumers, set up under the Act. They were expected to act as "nurses for private enterprises". They were also to function as a bridge to link the public and private sectors ensuring that the private industry obeys the rules of the game of planned economic development of the country. The act provides that the Central Government may establish for any scheduled industry or group of scheduled industries a Development Council. The functions of a development council are -

(i) Suggesting norms of efficiency by eliminating waste and reducing costs.

(ii) Recommending measures for improving the working of less efficient units of the industry.

(iii) Promoting marketing system which would help in satisfying the consumer.

(iv) Promoting standardization of products.

(v) Recommending production targets and reviewing progress from time to time.

(vi) Promoting the education and training of persons in technical or artistic subjects relevant to persons engaged in industry.

(vii) Promoting scientific and industrial research.

(viii) Promoting the adoption of measures for increasing the productivity of labour.

(ix) Promoting standardization of accounting and costing methods and practices.

(x) Advising the Central Government on matters relating to industry which the Central Government may request.

Functions of the IDR Act

Registration of undertakings: The IDR Act provides that all the industrial undertakings listed in the First Schedule of the Act should be registered with the Government. The Government will issue a certificate of registration which will contain the productivity capacity of the industry.

Industrial Licensing: After the commencement of the Act, no person or authority can establish any new industrial undertaking. The Government can however grant exemptions in this regard. Before the policy of liberalization, a license was required to establish a new undertaking manufacture a new item, substantially increase capacity of an industrial undertaking, change of location etc. However, the new industrial policy has abolished industrial licensing for all industries except 15 specified industries.

Power to Investigate fall in output etc.: The Act provides that a full and complete investigation may be made, if the Central Government, is of the opinion that there has been or is likely to be, an unjustifiable or a substantial fall in the output or a deterioration in the quality of the output or an unjustifiable rise in price. If, after such an investigation, the Central Government is satisfied that action is necessary, it may give appropriate directions to the concerned undertaking (sec 16).

If the industrial undertaking fails to comply with such directives, the Central Government is authorized to take over the control of the industry.

Power to take over Management: If the Central Government is of the opinion that any industrial undertaking is managed in a manner highly detrimental to the public interest, it may after a full and complete investigation, authorize any person to take over the management and control of the industry. Thus, the Central Government could take under its own management undertakings which failed to carry out its instructions for improvement in management and policies.

Power to Provide Relief to Certain Industrial Undertakings: The Act empowers the Central Government to provide certain relief to an industrial undertaking if the management or control has been taken over by the Government and if it is in the interest of the general public, with a view to preventing a fall in the volume of production of any schedule industry.

Price and Distribution Control: the act empowers the Government to prescribe prices, methods and the volume of production and channels of distribution. This is done with the objective of securing an equitable distribution and availability of the articles or class of articles at a fair price. The Government may notify the order under section 18-G of the Act.

Exemptions from the Act

Section 29-B of the Act empowers the Central Government to grant exemptions to this act, if the Central Government is of the opinion that it would not be in public interest to apply all or any of the provisions of the Act. The order of the Central Government may be notified in the Official Gazette.

Powers for Inspection: In order to ascertain the working of any industrial undertakings, the Central Government may authorize any person to -

(i) Enter and inspect any premises

(ii) Order the production of any document, book, register or record in their possession; and

(iii) Examine any person having the control of, or employed in connection with, any industrial undertaking.

INDUSTRIAL LICENSING IN INDIA

In order to accomplish the socio-economic goals embodied in the Industrial Policy Resolutions of 1948 and 1956, the industrial licensing system under the Industries Development and Regulation Act 1951 was established. An inter-ministerial licensing committee with the assistance of the Directorate General Technical Development was vested with power to issue industrial licenses. The prospective investor was to seek license from the Comptroller of Capital Issues, Capital Goods Committee and Foreign Agreement Committee to set up an industrial project.

It cannot be denied that since the system of industrial licensing was adopted, Indian industries have registered substantial progress in the desired directions. The industrial structure in India has become considerably diversified. Investment has been directed to new fields. There has also been remarkable growth of small industries and sectoral and regional imbalances with our industrial growth. The working of the industrial licensing system during the planning period revealed some major defects. It was criticized that industrial licensing system was promoting the interests of large business houses and it had led to inefficiency in industrial planning. Thus, it was felt that it required a careful look into the whole system. The actual operation of the system of industrial licensing of India has been evaluated by a number of official agencies.

(i) The Mahalonobis Committee (1960)

(ii) The Dasa Gupta Committee (1964)

(iii) The Hazari Committee Report (1966) and

(iv) The Subimal Dutt Report (1967)

1. The Mahalanobis Committee: The Planning Commission appointed the "Distribution of Income and Levels of Living Committee" under the chairmanship of Mahalanobis in 1960. The purpose of the Mahalonobis Committee was to inquire how the additional income generated in the First and Second Plans had been spread in the country. The Mahalanobis Committee which looked into the functioning of the economic system during the first decade of planning came out with the conclusion that the planned economic development contributed to the growth of big companies in the industrial sector. The concentration of wealth and power in big companies was caused, in the main, by the defective operation of industrial licensing and by liberal assistance of financial institutions of the companies. In view of the suggestions made by the Mahalonobies Committee that more comprehensive and detailed information regarding the many aspects and ramifications of economic power and control in the private sector be obtained, the Das Gupta Committee was appointed by the Central Government.

2. *The Das Gupta Committee Report:* A five member Monopolies Enquiry Commission under the chairmanship of Das Gupta was appointed by Central Government in April 1964. The Monopolies Enquiry Commission was entrusted with the task of Enquiry into 'the existence and effect of concentration of economic power in private hands'. The commission identified "product-wise" and "country-wise" concentration and attributed such concentration in the private sector to the process of industrialization. Further, the commission pointed out that concentration of economic power was on account of the advantage the big business had in securing industrial license for starting new industries or for expanding the capacity. The commission was convinced that the system of controls in the shape of industrial licensing restricted the freedom of entry into industry and so helped to produce concentration.

3. *The Hazari Committee Report:* In view of the disclosures made by the Dasa Gupta committee report. It was felt that the Industries (Development and Regulation) Act had not served its purpose fully. The Hazari Committee was therefore, appointed to review the operation of licensing under the Industries (Development and Regulation) Act. According to Hazari report, licensing system worked to the advantage of the big business houses. The big industrial houses obtained licenses easily, preventing the entry of new entrepreneurs.

This had resulted in the concentration of economic power in the hands of a few big industrial houses. Further, big houses followed the practice of putting in number of applications for each product and were able to obtain licenses. Therefore, the basic idea of a license, namely, social sanction for drawing scarce resources from the national pool, had not been fulfilled.

Findings of the Hazari Committee Report: The Commission of Enquiry under Dr. R.K. Hazari was appointed to review the working of industrial licensing under the I (D and R) Act, made some sensational disclosures. They are -

1. The licensing system did not provide automatically package sanction or clearance. Hence, there was inordinate delay in securing final permission.
2. Some leading houses followed the practice of multiple applications for the same product, and a wide variety of products, so as to produce more than the license capacity per unit. The Hazari Committee report clearly pointed out that the concerns on behalf of which licenses were applied were not necessarily very efficient and well managed industrial units. Some were brought into existence with the sole object of enabling business houses to put in applications.
3. For the purpose of sanctioning licenses, the principle of chronological selection i.e., first come first served basis was adopted. This resulted in big industrial houses to maintain offices in Delhi and put in their applications at the earliest opportunity, so that they could stand first in the queue. This procedure helped the big industrial houses. The Hazari report clearly pointed out -"It is perhaps, no accident that certain Birla Companies which appear repeatedly among the ranks of applicants".
4. The operation of licensing system failed to achieve

the objective of balanced regional development. According to the Hazari Committee report, "the gains in terms of balanced regional development and wider distribution of entrepreneurs are, at least, moderate. That licensing has served to canalise investment appears extremely doubtful". Thus the Hazari Committee has very clearly pointed out that Industrial Licensing did not bring about balanced regional development". It therefore recommended for through recast of the licensing system.

5. Many of the large industrial houses were guilty of non-implementation. The most disappointing feature was that the authorities concerned were not even aware of the total investment and foreign exchange commitments of licenses issued or those under implementation at any particular period of time. Thus, there was total failure of comprehensive planning and absence of follow up action once the license was issued.

To sum up, therefore, the licensing policy projected an exaggerated picture of industrial capacity. In the absence of a policy of revocation of licenses issued, the large industrial houses prevented the entry of new entrepreneurs. They did not even fulfil the targets laid down in the plan. Consequently, industrial licensing which was supposed to act as an instrument of industrial development became an impediment. Therefore, the Hazari Committee suggested to recast the scope and working of the licensing system.

4. Dutt Committee Report: Following a discussion of the Hazari Committee report in Parliament, the Government of India appointed a committee under the chairmanship of Mr. Subimal Dutt in July 1967. The committee submitted its report in July 1969.

Principal findings of the Dutt Committee

The Dutt Committee enquire into the working of the industrial licensing system over the 10 year period 1956-66 and brought out several deficiencies and malpractices. It was founded out that in the case of 51 products; the large industrial houses controlled 50% of the licenses. Attempt was not made to control the further growth of these big houses. Besides, more than 31.8% of the licenses issued in the 10 year period were not implemented. This non-implementation had serious impact on industrial growth. Some industrial houses indulged in submitting multiple applications for the same product through various firms under their control. Besides, the licensing system did not help in the attainment of objective of import substitution. In many cases, the objective of regional dispersal of industries was overlooked for example Maharastra, West Bengal, Gujarat and Tamil Nadu was able to acquire 62% of the total licenses issued. On the basis of "common authority" and "controlling interest" represented by effective equity of one-third, the Dutt Committee, has classified big business into 73 large industrial houses and 60 independent concerns. It has reveled that the principle of first come first served' for issuing licenses enabled the big business with advantage to foreclose the licensing capacity. Big business houses, accounted for disproportionately larger share in the total licenses granted, in the total investment on plant and machinery, in the total financial assistance by the term lending institutions. Of the loan assistance granted to the large industrial sector, 44% had gone to the 73 large houses. Also, they were issued licenses to operate in the fields reserved for the State.

Dutt Committee's conclusions on the grant of Industrial Licensing

The Dutt Committee came to the following conclusions on the grant of industrial licensing.

i) *Abuses of the system of licenses:* The Dutt Committee made a very serious indictment on the working of industrial licensing in the country. Industrial licensing was designed to bring about reduction in or at least put a restraint on the growing concentration of economic power with the large business houses. But this did not happen.

ii) *Large share of Licenses for Big Industrial Houses:* The large industrial houses, accounted for 41% in the total proposed investment on machinery and for 40% of the total approved import of capital goods. Further more, 60% of the value of import of capital goods by the entire private sector was accounted for by 73 large industrial houses.

iii) *Failure in achieving Balanced Regional Development:* The Industrial Licensing system was unable to help the industrially backward states. It was found out by the Dutt Committee that the 4 industrially advanced states of Maharastra, West Bengal, Gujarat and Tamil Nadu were able to acquire 62% of the total licenses issued. Even Product wise distribution of licenses also revealed a high degree of concentration in the already industrialized states.

iv) *Large amount of licenses granted to Private Sector:* Licenses were freely granted to the private sector. In the Machine Tools industry, only 9 licenses were given to the Public Sector HMT whereas, 226 licenses were issued to the private sector. In the aluminium industries, the entire development was permitted in the private sector, though the development of aluminium industries was to be the responsibility of the public sector. Similarly, in the case of synthetic rubber and chemical pulp, all the licenses were allotted to the private sector. In fertilizers, 42 licenses were granted to the private sector in comparison to 12 licenses issued to the public sector. Thus, we can conclude that the Licensing System granted license to the private sector under one pretext or the other. Further more even the area reserved for the public sector was not spared.

v) *Large Share of Financial Assistance to Big Business Houses:* The Dutt Committee made an analysis of the financial assistance provided by financial institutions. Even the public sector financial institutions like UTI and LIC did not provide any financial assistance to the public sector. The 20 large industrial houses, received nearly 43% of the total funds loaned out by these financial institutions. Even the Banking institutions showed a heavy preference for large industrial houses. The large industrial houses received 71% of the total financial assistance given by the banking institutions to industries. Thus, we can conclude that the various financial institutions showed a distinct preference for the large industrial houses.

vi) *Unjustified Foreign Collaboration in Non-Essential Consumer Goods:* Foreign collaboration were permitted in non-essential items like refrigerators, radio receivers, toilet soap, ball point pens etc. This approach of the Government was unsolicited and unjustifiable besides being a heavy strain on the scarce foreign exchange resources of the country.

It is thus clear from the above mentioned facts that the industrial licensing system failed to achieve the objective of planned economic development as well as of preventing concentration of economic power. The situation forestalled the entry of new entrepreneurs and thus failed to help the medium and small entrepreneurs. Further more, the licensing system also did not help in balanced regional development of the industrial structure.

Recommendations of the Dutt Committee

The Dutt Committee recommendations were aimed at reconciling the objectives of economic development and legality in the framework of the mixed economy as visualized by our planners. The following are the recommendations of the Dutt Committee.

1. While issuing licenses to the industrial units, in addition to the objective of the economic development, even the goal of removing concentration of economic power must be satisfied. The Dutt Committee recommended the setting up of monopolies commission with sufficient powers to deal with the problems of concentration of economic power or product monopolies.
2. The Dutt Committee also recommended the classification of industries into core sector, non-core sector, and reserved sector and so on. The Government accepted these recommendations.
3. The Dutt Committee recommended permission to large industrial houses to enter the core sector so as to utilize large funds which these industrial houses had accumulated and which they were eager to invest in articles of non-essential consumption catering to the demand of the few rich in the society. This recommendation of the Dutt Committee which was accepted by the Government scrapped at one stroke the arguments advanced for the reservation of industries of basic and strategic importance in the public sector.
4. The Dutt Committee wanted the Indian Bureaucracy to harmonize the social interest with the private

interest. Experience has shown that a very strong nexus has developed between industrial houses, politicians and bureaucracy.

5. The working of the public sector financial institutions also favoured big houses in the matter of credit and loans. Dutt Committee recommended a change in the basis of financial institutions.

On the basis of these recommendations the Government announced new licensing policy in 1970.

NEW LICENSING POLICY AND PROCEDURES, 1970

In the light of Dutt Committee's recommendations, the Government announced a new policy on 18th February 1970.

1. According to this new policy, industries were divided into three parts:

(a) Core-sector industries consisting of basic and strategic industries like atomic energy, cement, iron and steel etc., would continue to be developed exclusively in the public sector. These industries require assets of Rs.5 crore or more.

(b) Middle or decentralized industries which are non-reserved are left open to private entrepreneurs. These industries require investment of Rs. 1 crore to Rs.5 crore.

(c) Non-core heavy investment sector or joint sector consists of those industries which require assets of more than 5 crores.

The policy permitted the private sector to participate in the establishment of industries in the non-core heavy investment sector except in scheduled industries.

2. The new licensing policy laid down that preference

would be given to the co-operative sector in the matter of licensing new agro-industries.

3. The new-licensing policy, considered small-scale sector as unlicensed. Small-sector was defined as one with industries having fixed investment below Rs.7 lakhs.

4. The policy provides a wider scope for the expansion of the public sector.

The prevalent licensing system was entirely unsatisfactory and failed to fulfill the objectives of government's industrial policy and plan priorities. Therefore, some changes were made in licensing policy in 1973, 1975 and 1980.

INDUSTRIAL LICENSING POLICY, 1973

Important modifications were made in the licensing policy in February, 1973. The important modifications were as follows:

(a) Larger houses with assets of not less than Rs.20 crores were made eligible to participate in and contribute to the establishment of such industries along with other applicants. However, the items reserved for production in the public sector, or in the small sector, large business houses were not permitted.

(b) The Government would develop joint sector as a promotional instrument in priority areas.

(c) Limit in the value of assets was lowered from Rs.35 crores to Rs.20 crores. These changes gave a considerable concession to private sector and foreign multinationals.

(d) Co-operatives and small and medium entrepreneurs were to be encouraged to participate in the production of mass consumption of goods.

INDUSTRIAL LICENSING POLICY 1975

In October 1975, the Government announced major changes liberalizing industrial licensing policy. The important modifications were as follows: -

(a) It was decided to exempt from the normal industrial licensing procedure, medium entrepreneurs to enable them to set up industrial capacities based on indigenous equipment and local raw materials and also to utilize to a fuller extent the existing installed capacities.

(b) It delicensed 21 industries and permitted unlimited expansion beyond the licensed capacities.

(c) Although in the large-scale sector, industrial licensing has not been formally withdrawn, but in actual practice the industrial houses create unauthorized capacities which are later ratified by the government. This was done with objective to raise production.

INDUSTRIAL LICENSING POLICY 1980

The Government made some changes in Industrial Licensing Policy in July 1980. The changes were: -

1. The Industrial units which had exceeded their licensed capacity got not only the excess regularized, but also further liberalized in the interest of raising industrial production.
2. Several industries which were important from the point of view of national economy could not increase their capacity because of the constraints imposed on them. The new policy recognized and endorsed such enhanced production potential.

INDUSTRIAL LICENSING POLICY 1982

The Government made some changes in the Industrial Licensing Policy, 1982. These changes removed some of the serious anomalies in the industrial policy. The important changes are as follows: -

1. Some key industries of national importance were exempted from the rigorous provisions of the MRTP Act.
2. Foreign investors could now raise their equity investment above the 40% prescribed by FERA, where technology was used to manufacture goods meant for export.
3. The MRTP Act was amended to streamline the procedure involved in industrial licensing so that bureaucratic delays would be removed.
4. In order to promote exports, while issuing industrial licenses, to MRTP units, the determinations of 'dominance' has been relaxed.

LIBERALIZATION MEASURES 1985 AND 1986

The Rajiv Gandhi's Government brought about a sea-change in terms of liberalization of Industrial Licensing Policy. The major changes were as follows: -

1. The ILP 85 made some changes in favour of big houses in terms of making them free from the provisions of MRTP Act and FERA.
2. In order to encourage production, "broad banding" was introduced in items like machine tools, paper pulp, motorized two wheelers etc.
3. Licenses issued in terms of this broad banding would enable a given undertaking to produce any type of item covered as long as the total production did not exceed the overall licensed capacity.

4. The threshold asset limit for companies under MRTP Act was raised from Rs.20 crores to Rs.100 crores.
5. The Government exempted 27 industries from section 22A of the MRTP Act.
6. The industrial licensing proposals above an investment of Rs.50 crores (as against the earlier laid limit of Rs.20 crores) would have to be cleared by the cabinet committee on Economic Affairs.
7. The limit on investment by small-scale units was enhanced from Rs.20 lakhs to Rs.35 lakhs and in the case of ancillaries it was enhanced from 25 lakhs to 45 lakhs.

In 1986, the following measures were introduced: -

1. The Government decided to delicense 23 industries for MRTP and FERA Companies provided the industrial undertaking is located in any of the centrally-declared backward areas.
2. The Government decided to allow industrial undertakings to freely produce in excess of licensed capacity by 10%, if the additional production is exported.

INDUSTRIAL LICENSING 1988

In 1988, the Government announced further liberalization of the licensing system. The changes were -

1. Non MRTP and non FERA companies are exempted from obtaining licenses for projects involving investment in fixed assets upto Rs.50 crores. If they are located in backward areas and upto Rs.15 crores if they are located in non-backward areas.
2. In order to fulfill the objectives of more production, the Government allowed large industrial units by

providing licenses for substantial expansion, new articles etc.

3. To promote industrialization in backward areas, new industrial undertakings established in declared backward areas, are entitled to the income tax relief under section 80 HH of the Income Tax Act by way of deduction of 20% of the profits available for a period of 10 years.

INDUSTRIAL LICENSING 1991

In 1991, the Government announced further liberalization of the licensing system. The changes introduced in 1991 were:

1. The licensing system for all industries other than those given in Annex II was scrapped. These industries are coal, petroleum, distillation and brewing of alcoholic drinks, sugar, cigars and cigarettes, motor cars, plywood, hazardous chemicals,, drugs and pharmaceuticals, entertainment electronic, air conditioners, refrigerators and domestic washing machines.
2. The compulsory licensing provisions would not apply to any of such items which are reserved for small scale sector.

To conclude, we can say that by allowing large industrial units' licenses for substantial expansion, new articles etc., the Government might fulfil the objective of more production but, the de-reservation has hit the small-scale sector. As a result, the objective of promoting full employment by encouraging small sector will be jeopardized. Further, the licensing policy has failed to achieve the other objectives such as checking concentration of economic power, balanced regional development etc.

QUESTIONS

1. Give a critical account of the Industrial Licensing Policy in India.
2. What is Industrial Licensing Policy? Explain the main provisions of the Industrial (development and regulation) Act 1951.
3. Mention the findings of the Hazari Committee Report.

UNIVERSITY QUESTIONS

(15 Marks)

- What is Industrial Licensing Policy? Explain the main provisions of the Industries Development and Regulation Act 1951 (October 2002) (October 1996)

(1 Mark)

- Subimal Dutt Report (October/ November 2004)
- Hazare Report (April 2004)
- Tiny Sector (April/May 2003)
- Give the capital limit of small scale ancillaries and tiny sectors .(October 2002)
- Mention any two recommendations of Dutt Committee Report. .(October 2002) (October 1996)

7

BUSINESS AND PUBLIC

Learning Objectives

After going through this chapter, you will be conversant with:

Business and elements in its environment:

- Stockholders
- Customers
- Employees
- Labour Organisations
- Financial Institutions
- Suppliers
- Competitors
- Government

A business will encounter many interest groups in its environment. According to Philip Kotler - "A public is any group that has an actual or potential interest in or impact on an organizations ability to achieve its interests". Business units are the creation of society. The business enterprises therefore have to function by keeping in mind the interests of society. They have to consider the interests of the consumers, shareholders, employees, government and society. These elements effect the business organization and influence management policies and strategies.

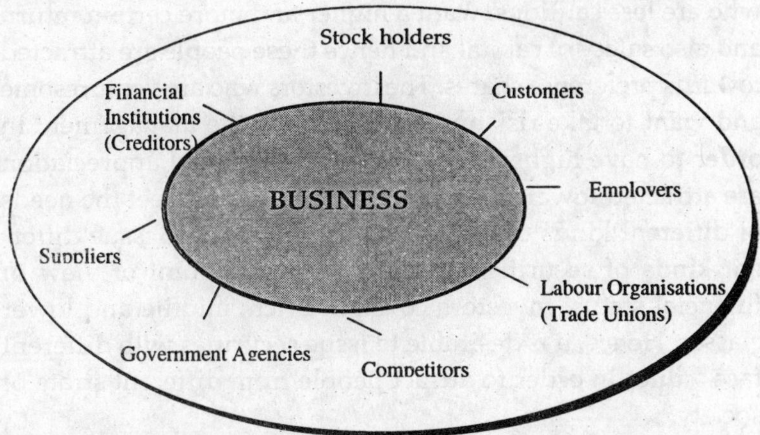

Fig 7.1. Business firm and elements in its environment.

The various elements that influence the business are discussed below

1. STOCKHOLDERS

The shareholders are the persons who provide the funds to the business enterprise. The business should be managed efficiently so as to provide a fair return on the investments of the shareholders. They should be provided with comprehensive reports giving full information about its working. In the same way, the shareholders should also meet the obligations of the business enterprise by supporting the efforts of the business so that continuous development of the enterprise is possible. They should encourage the business to follow a dynamic policy and to plough back profit for the purpose of development and expansion.

Needs of the Investors: Investors are of different types. Some are cautious, some are less cautious and some are venturesome. The investors who are cautious care more for security of the principal and stability of income and hence generally they are attracted towards debentures. The investors, who are less cautious, want a higher and more certain return and also safety of capital and hence these people are attracted towards preference shares. The investors who are venturesome and want to take risk and participate in the management in order to have higher income as well as capital appreciation are attracted towards equity shares. Hence to meet the needs of different kinds of investors it is necessary to issue different kinds of securities. Further, from the point of view of financial status, investors consist of rich, middle and lower classes. Hence, it is desirable to issue securities with different face values in order to attract people from different strata of society.

Sources of Finance: A business enterprise requires two types of capital namely, fixed capital and working capital. Fixed capital is needed for acquiring various fixed assets like land, building, land and machinery, furniture etc. It includes long term financing and is raised from the capital markets. It can be raised from the following sources -

(a) Shareholders;

(b) Debenture holders;

(c) Financial Institutions and

(d) Retained earnings or Ploughing back of Profits.

Here we will discuss, (a) (b) and (d) as all these three sources come from the investing public. (c) Will be discussed under the heading financial institutions which will be discussed in the subsequent part of this chapter.

(a)Shareholders: Issue of ownership securities (shares) is the most important method of raising long-term or permanent capital required by the business. A share is a unit of member's interest in the company's capital. The share capital of a company is divided into a large number of equal parts. Each part is known as a share. A share may be in the form of

bearer security i.e., share-warrant. There are three types of shares - equity or ordinary shares, preference shares and deferred shares. Shares are ownership securities. The Issue of ownership securities is the most important method of raising permanent capital required by a business.

Under the Companies Act 1956, a company can issue two types of ownership securities, namely equity shares and preference shares.

Equity Shares: Shares which are not preference shares are known as equity shares or ordinary shares. The dividend on these shares is paid after the dividend on preference shares has been paid. The rate of dividend on such shares depends upon the amount of profits available and the intention of directors. These shares have the chance of earning good dividends and also run the risk of receiving nothing. If the company goes into liquidation, the amount of equity capital will be repayable only after every claim has been settled. Therefore, equity share capital is referred to as 'venture capital'.

Features of Equity Shares

(a) *Risk Capital*: Equity shareholders have an unlimited interest in the company's profits and assets. The prospects raise or fall with the prosperity of their company. Therefore, equity is also called as 'risk' or 'venture' capital.

(b) *Fluctuating Dividend*: If the profits are substantial, equity shareholders may get good dividends, if not, there may be little or no dividend. Thus, dividend is of fluctuating character.

(c) *Voting Right*: Equity shareholders enjoy a statutory right to vote in the general meeting of the company. His voting right is governed by the articles of association. One share has one vote. Thus, the voting right of a shareholder depends on the number of shares held by him.

(d) *Changing market value*: The market value of ordinary shares depends mainly on the profit earned by the company, dividend prospects, the quality and caliber of management and general business outlook.

Preference Shares: Preference shareholders have a preferential right to receive dividend and also a preferential right to receive back the capital in the event of dissolution, if there is any surplus. Preference shares suit the investors who want a limited but steady return on his money.

Features of Preference Shares

(a) *Return of Income*: They have the first preference to share in the profits among all shareholders.

(b) *Return of Capital*: At the time of winding up of the company, they have the first preference to get back their capital, among all shareholders.

(c) *Fixed Dividend*: They are fixed-income securities. According to the terms of issue and the Articles of Association, the preference shareholders shall have a fixed rate of dividend. On account of fixed dividends, these shares cannot have any chance to share in the prosperity of the company's business.

(d) *Non-participation in Management*: Preference shareholders do not enjoy normal voting rights except when their interests are being directly affected. Thus, they do not have any voice in the management of the company.

Types of Preference Shares: Preference shares may be divided into the following types or classes. They are

(i) *Cumulative Preference Shares:* Cumulative preference shareholders are entitled to arrears of dividend on their shares to be paid out of profits of subsequent years, if in any year the dividend on them could not be paid due to lack of profits. Thus, the dividend goes on accumulating if it is not paid and should be paid in the subsequent years when the company makes profits.

(ii) *Non-Cumulative Preference Shares*: Unlike cumulative preference shareholders, the non-cumulative preference share holders do not get arrears of dividend and hence dividend not paid will not accumulate. If, there is unpaid dividend in any year it will not be paid out of the future profits of the company.

(iii) *Participating Preference Shares*: Participating preference shareholders have the right to participate in profits, if there is any balance after paying dividend on preference shares and equity shares.

(iv) *Redeemable Preference Shares*: Redeemable preference shares are shares which will be repaid on or after a certain date.

(v) *Convertible Preference Shares*: Convertible preference shareholders have a right to convert their shares into equity shares according to the terms of issue. This option has to be exercised within a fixed period.

(vi) *Non-convertible Preference Shares*: Unlike convertible preference shareholders, these shareholders do not have any right to convert their shares into equity shares.

Difference between Preference shares and Equity shares

PREFERENCE SHARES	*EQUITY SHARES*
1. They enjoy first preference in getting dividend.	1. Their claim to receive dividend is secondary and if there is surplus profit.
2. They enjoy first right to receive back their capital in case of dissolution.	2. They rank next to preference shares in the return of capital.

3. Dividend rate fixed by Articles of Association, unpaid dividends can accumulate if they are cumulative preference shares.	3. Dividend rate fluctuates according to the earning power of the company. Equity shares are always non-cumulative.
4. They are entitled to enjoy voting right only under exceptional circumstances and can vote on resolutions effecting their rights.	4. They enjoy normal voting rights. Voting rights is in proportion to the paid up amount in shares.
5. Face value is relatively higher.	5. Face value is relatively lower.
6. Preference shares can be redeemable at the end of a certain period.	6. Equity shares are always irredeemable and they constitute a permanent share capital of the company.
7. Preference shares involve a small risk and their rights are secured. Hence they appeal to cautious investors.	7. The equity share capital have too bear the risk of loss in expectation of higher and raising dividends. Hence they appeal to investors who prefer risking though unstable income.
8. No capital appreciation as no chance to share in company's prosperity.	8. Capital appreciation possible due to prospects of rising dividends.

(b) Debenture Holders: Debentures are creditorship securities which provide funds to the company on loan basis rather than on capital basis. A debenture is an instrument of credit, a bond of indebtedness or a mere acknowledgement of debt, issued by a company under its common seal. It is a loan or borrowed capital of the company. It acts as an external source of finance. It contains a contract for repayment of the borrowed amount. E.g.: after 5 or 7 or 10 years and for payment of interest, usually half-yearly at a fixed rate until the repayment of the loan. If the interest and/or principal is unpaid, the

debenture holders (if they are mortgage debentures) can sell up the property and repay themselves from the proceeds of the sale of assets.

The debentures can be issued at any time. The Articles usually empower the board of directors to issue debentures. The board cannot issue debentures if the amount already borrowed by the company exceeds its paid up capital and free reserves. For issuing any excess debentures, the board must get the sanction of the members at the general meeting.

Kinds of Debentures

1. *Secured and Simple Debentures*: On the basis of security, the debentures may be secured or unsecured. In the case of secured debentures (also called mortgage debentures) the property or assets of the company are mortgaged as security. The debenture-holders are secured creditors of the company.

In case of unsecured or simple or naked debentures, no such mortgage of property takes place and the debenture holders are unsecured creditors of the company.

2. *Redeemable and Perpetual Debentures*: On the basis of period of repayment, the debentures may be redeemable or irredeemable. Redeemable debentures are paid out of a special reserve fund created for the purpose. Irredeemable debentures may not be repaid in the life-time of the company.

3. *Registered and Bearer Debentures*: On the basis of transferability we have registered or bearer debentures. In the case of registered debentures, the company has to maintain a Register of debenture-holders in which particulars of the debenture holder like name and addresses are recorded. Such debentures are transferred through a regular instrument of transfer which is duly signed by the seller as well as buyer. The instrument of transfer duly signed and together with the original debenture certificate should be placed before the

directors for their approval. When the directors pass the transfer of debentures the seller's name is removed from the Register and the buyer's name is entered there in. A new debenture certificate is issued to the buyer.

The bearer debenture is regarded as a negotiable instrument (just like a bearer cheque). It is transferable for bearer. The company does not maintain any Register of debenture-holders. The ownership of a bearer debenture can pass from person to person merely by delivery.

Difference between Shares and Debentures

SHARES	*DEBENTURES*
1. A share indicates ownership. The shareholder is the member of a company.	1. A debenture indicates creditorship. The debenture holder is the creditor of the company.
2. A shareholder gets dividend when the company makes profit. The payment of dividend is not compulsory.	2. A debenture-holder gets interest at the fixed rate irrespective of profit or loss made by the company. The payment of interest is compulsory.
3. Amount of share is never to be repaid except when company is too be wound up.	3. Amount of debenture (except irredeemable debentures) is to be repaid usually at the end of a fixed period.
4. At the time of winding up share holders will get their repayment only if there is a surplus and after all the creditors are repaid in full	4. At the time of winding up debenture holders will enjoy the right of priority in repayment of their capital.
5. The rights and privileges of shareholders are described in the articles of association.	5. The rights and privileges of debenture holders are defined in the debenture certificate.
6. Issue of shares at a premium at a discount is subject to certain legal restrictions.	6. Debentures can be issued either at a premium or at a discount without restrictions.

(c) Retained Earnings: Ploughing back of profits is a commonly used method by established business units. It is also called 'internal financing' and 'self-financing'. When a company retains a portion of the distributable profits in the form of free reserves and utilizes this amount for further expansion, it is called ploughing back of profits.

Advantages of Ploughing Back of Profits

1. It is a cost free source of finance because there is no direct cost on retained profits, there is no cost of raising capital and there is no compulsory payment of interest.

2. There is no pledge, no mortgage, when we have self-financing.

3. It is very convenient source of finance. There is no waste of time in planning the sale of securities.

4. There is no change in control because we do not have increase in the equity capital and owners are completely free from outside control because there is no debenture or share issue.

5. If a country wants accelerated economic development and capital formation, the practice of self-financing of growth and expansion will be socially desirable.

Disadvantages of Ploughing-back of Profits

1. Danger of misuse of funds.

2. Danger of overcapitalization due to frequent issue of bonus shares.

3. Changing shareholders not interested in ploughing back of profits as they get lower dividends.

4. Danger of manipulation of share value by management.

5. Tendency towards monopoly due to over investment.

Responsibility towards investors: It is the primary responsibility of the business to see that its investors get a fair return on the capital which he invests. The reasonable and lawful expectations of the investors should be rationally analyzed and assessed. If conditions are created which do not ensure such security, then the inevitable consequence is flight of capital, withdrawal of capital and search for alternative investments.

2. CUSTOMERS

Customers' satisfaction is the ultimate aim of all economic activity. This involves more than the offer of products at the lowest possible price. Adulteration of goods, poor quality, failure to give fair service, misleading advertising etc are some of the violation by business towards its customers. A business enterprise has positive responsibility towards the consumers of its products. It has to provide quality goods to customers at the right time, right place, and at right price. It must guard the consumers against the poor quality of goods, incorrect measures, poor after-sale service, adulteration of goods, misleading advertisements, lack of courtesy to customers and restrictive trade practices. The general feeling is that the business community has not discharged these responsibilities satisfactorily. The areas of failure are -

(a) Price level.

(b) Poor service.

(c) Low quality and standard.

(a) *Price level*: It is the responsibility of a business to ensure that goods are available at fair, reasonable and relatively stable prices. The general impression is that the business is by and large responsible for the raising prices. Hoarding and cornering leads to rise in prices.

(b)*Poor service*: A business should provide good after sale services. In other words, the sale should be followed by service to ensure advice, guidance and maintenance. But unfortunately, in many business organizations the relationship between them and the customers comes to an end with the sale. This attitude should be reversed.

(c) *Low quality and standard*: Business enterprise should give adequate attention to quality and standard. Compulsory quality control is necessary to ensure good quality. it is widely felt that the quality of goods is low because

- The method of manufacture is not standardized.
- Low quality of labour.
- Inefficiency of supervision and control.
- Lack of response towards established standards of quality.

The Justice Mukherji Report to the Calcutta Seminar on social responsibility of business has suggested measures to improve the quality and standards. The same is reproduced here below :

(i) Every manufacturer should have a quality control section, either at the unit level or group or association level;

(ii) Different trade associations should prepare suitable and detailed specifications of the products or goods manufactured / marketed by their members;

(iii) Every article manufactured should pass the quality tests at different stages of manufacturing before it finally goes out of the factory. Where the unit level quality control section is not available suitable sampling methods should be adopted and such samples should be tested at the group or the association level;

(iv) Marketing associations in charge of general administration of organized markets and market places, including Government, municipal and corporation markets should set up vigilance over traders operating in such markets, to ensure fair practice in regard to quality, prices and other terms of the trade.

(v) Businessmen themselves should form voluntary associations of permanent nature to exercise effective checks on their members by setting up disciplinary committees, as in other professions, with powers to boycott or blacklist members found guilty of malpractice in the matter of quality of goods supplied and thereby dissuade the general public from dealing with such business.

Thus, every business enterprise should provide its customers with -

- Goods to meet the needs of consumers of different classes and tastes.
- Price the goods reasonably.
- Make goods of dependable quality.
- Ensure after-sales service.
- Provide sufficient variety of goods.

3. EMPLOYEES

Employees should be treated as human beings and their cooperation must be achieved for the realization of the business enterprises goals. The responsibilities of the business enterprises to its employees are - the security of employment with fair wages, equal opportunity for growth and development within the organization, fair promotions, employee welfare, social security and profit sharing. Further, the business enterprise should also provide the employee welfare, social security and profit sharing. Further, the business enterprise should also provide the employees scope for improvement of educational qualification, training and upgrading of skills so that they may get a chance to improve their prospects.

Importance of Employees to a Business Enterprise: The importance of employees to a business enterprise can be viewed from three stand points –

(a) Social Significance: Every business enterprise is a part of society and hence it must look at every step it takes from the point of view of the requirements of society. Proper management of personnel enhances their dignity by satisfying their social needs. It can strive to achieve this by-

- Providing suitable and most productive employment which will bring the employees psychological satisfaction.
- By paying the employee a reasonable compensation in proportion to the contribution made by him.
- Eliminating improper use of human resources.
- By helping people make their own decisions in matters which directly concern them.
- Maintaining a balance between the jobs available and the job seekers according to the qualifications and needs.

(b) Professional Significance: The dignity of employees as professionals and more importantly as human beings should be maintained. This can be achieved by providing a healthy work environment. In order to provide a healthy work environment, a business enterprise should provide:

- Maximum opportunities for personal development.
- Improving the employees working skill and capacity.

- By proper allocation of work and
- Maintaining the dignity of the employee as a "human being".

(c) *Significance for the individual business enterprise:* By treating the employees with dignity and by satisfying the social needs of its employees, a business enterprise not only does social service but also helps the organization to accomplish its own goals. This happens as a by product of an business enterprise's own initiative by -

- Securing willing co-operation of the employees for achieving goals of the business enterprise.
- Utilizing effectively the available human resources.
- Creating right attitude among the employees through effective motivation.

Role of a Business Organization towards its Employees

In the modern era, the management of the business organization usually performs a variety of roles in accordance with the needs of the employees as well as the needs of the situation -

- The business organization should have a humanitarian approach and discharge its moral and ethical obligations.
- The management should play the role of a mentor and counsellor to whom the employees feel free to approach to discuss their personal as well as career problems.
- The management should play the role of a mediator and offer to settle the disputes among individuals and groups.

The role of the organization towards its employees is ever expanding. The following chart explains the multifaceted role of a business organization towards its employees.

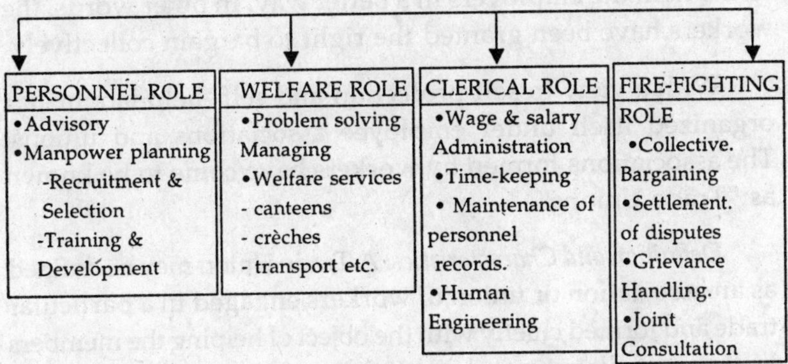

Fig. 7.2. Role of a business enterprise towards its employees.

Lapses on the part of the Business Enterprise towards its employees:

- Unsympathetic treatment of employees by the managers.
- Favouritism by management in giving increment, promotion and appointment.
- Lack of communication between employers and employees.
- Lack of leave facilities.
- Delay in settlement of disputes.
- Lack in welfare facilities for employees.

4. LABOUR ORGANIZATIONS (TRADE UNIONS)

Workers are poor and hence they cannot afford to remain without job for a long period. Most of them are ignorant and require advice and guidance from persons who have the genuine interest of the workers at heart. Each worker by himself is unable to fight against the injustice done to him.

As such all the economists have recognized the right of the workers to organize themselves. As a group they can settle terms with the employers in a better way. In other words, the workers have been granted the right to bargain collectively.

With a view to self-protection and self -help labour has organized itself under employee associations and unions. The associations formed by workers have come to be known as "Trade Unions".

Definition and Characteristics: A Trade Union may be defined as an association or union of workers engaged in a particular trade and formed chiefly with the object of helping the members in times of distress and getting the grievances settled and legitimate rights established.

According to section 2(b) of the Trade Unions Act of 1926 " A Trade Union is any combination of persons, whether temporary or permanent, primarily for the purpose of regulating the relations between workers and employers or between workers and workers and for imposing restrictive conditions on the conduct of any Trade or business and includes the federation of two or more trade unions".

From the definition we can arrive at the following features of a Trade Union:

1. Trade Union is an association, either of employees or employers or of independent workers.
2. It is relatively a permanent combination of workers engaged in securing socio-economic benefits for its members.
3. The nature and character of Trade Union has been constantly changing.
4. Its origin and growth has been influenced by a number of ideologies etc.

On the basis of the above features, we may define Trade Union as "A Continuous and Voluntary Association of the salary or wage earners and engaged in whatever industry or trade, formed for safeguarding the interests of its members, maintaining and improving the conditions of their working lives, raising their status and promoting their vocational interests and securing better relations between them and their employers through collective bargaining".

Thus, Trade Union is a device which enables a group or class in an industry to trade or bargain with any other class or group on equal footing. Such a union is,

1. Economically oriented.
2. An instrument of defence against exploitation;
3. An outcome of industrialization and implies class distinctation.

Principles of Trade Unionism: Trade Union functions on the basis of three traditional principles. If any one of them is threatened or is in jeopardy, they would fight back. These principles are:

1. Unity is strength.
2. Equal pay for equal work or for equal pay for the same job.
3. Security of service (both socio-economic).

Objectives of Trade Unions: The following are some of the aims and objectives of trade unions:

1. To secure for the workers fair wages in the light of cost of living and the prevailing standard of living in the country.
2. To improve the workers working conditions by securing shorter working hours, better leave facilities,

adequate social security benefits, appropriate educational facilities and other welfare benefits.

3. To assure the workers a share in the increased profitability of an industrial unit by providing him payment of adequate bonus.
4. To protect the workers interest and more specifically to avoid their exploitation (misuse or impropriety).
5. To ensure the workers security of employment by resisting retrenchment and victimization likely to harm them.
6. To protect the larger interest of society by aiding in the improvement of trade and industry etc.

Functions of Trade Union: Broadly speaking, the functions of the modern trade unions are very comprehensive. The functions of Trade Unions are generally classified into:

1. Militant or protective
2. Fraternal, ministrant or positive.

Under the former group of functions, a Trade Union is primarily concerned with obtaining better working conditions and of employment for its members through such militant activities as strikes and boycotts, which are generally resorted to when efforts at collective bargaining fail to bear results. The latter functions relate to the provision of benefits such as sickness and accident payments. A trade Union also offers financial assistance to its members during periods of temporary unemployment.

According to Trade Union Act of 1926 - "A Trade Union must work to protect and promote the interest of the workers and the conditions of their employment". The interest of the workers lies in getting reasonable wages, shorter working hours, improved working conditions - socio-economic and psychological and greater security; both to person and of the job.

The Advantages of Trade Unions: From the objects it is clear that there are certain benefits offered by trade unions. The good influences are:

1. Trade Unions today can get the best professional assistance. They are thus in a position to meet the employer on an equal footing.
2. They can induce the spirit of self-reliance and self-respect among the workers thereby helping to build-up national character. No self respecting worker wants gifts or alms but must be paid a fair share of the results based on the actual work produced.
3. As unions act as an organized body, the workers can negotiate with the employer on the basis of status and self-respect. Pressure can be brought by them on the employer to ensure that the factories are maintained in a healthy condition and that the hours of work are arranged conveniently. In case of grievance, the case can be presented through the union, thereby preventing unnecessary strife and disruption of work and
4. Trade Unions help in maintaining the wages at a uniform level in terms of the actual economic value.

Industrial Relations

The expression "Industrial Relations" is used to express the nature of relationship between the employer and employee in an industry or an organization. Where, willing co-operation emanates from employees towards the achievement of organizational goals, then, there is said to be good industrial relations.

However, "Industrial Relations" pose one of the most delicate problems to modern complex industrial society. The Industrial Relations can also often be identified with labour (employee) relations, personnel relations, employer-employee relationship etc. Industrial-relations are that aspect of management which deals with manpower or human resources (of all grades from Director to the machine operator).

Definition of Industrial Relations: "Industrial Relations" refer " to a dynamic and developing concept, which is not limited to the complex relations between Trade Unions and management but also refers to the general web of relationship normally obtained between employers and employees - a web much more complex than the simple concept of labour-capital conflict".

Under the heading "Industrial-Relations" the ILO (International Labour Organization) has dealt with the relationships between the state on the one hand and the employers' and employees' organizations (unions) on the other or with the relationships among the occupational organizations themselves. Thus, it involves a study of the state, the legal system, the worker's and employer's organizations at the institutional level; and of the patterns of industrial organization (including management), capital structure (including technology), compensation of the labour force, and the study of the market forces - all at the economic level.

Causes of poor Industrial Relations

There are many causes which have led to poor industrial relations and even generate good industrial relations. Perhaps, the main cause or source of poor industrial relations resulting in inefficiency and labour unrest is mental laziness on the part of both management and labour. However, the following are briefly the causes of poor industrial relations-

1. Mental inertia and the contempt on the part of management and labour.
2. An intolerant attitude of contempt towards the workers on the part of management.
3. Inadequate fixation of wage and wage-structure.
4. Unhealthy working conditions.
5. Indiscipline.
6. Lack of human relations skill on the part of supervisors and other managers.
7. Desire on the part of the workers for higher bonus, DA and corresponding desire of the employers to give as little as possible.
8. Inappropriate introduction of automation (mechanization) without providing the right climate.
9. Unduly heavy work load.
10. Dispute on sharing the gains of the productivity.
11. Unfair labour practices - victimization, undue dismissal, and lock-outs.

Industrial Relations, therefore, do not constitute a simple relationship, but are a set of functional, inter-dependent complexities involving historical, economic, social, psychological, demographic, technological, occupational, political, legal and other variables etc.

Objectives of Industrial Relations: The primary objective of industrial relations is to bring about healthy and cordial relations between employees and employers. An industry is a social world in miniature. As an association of various persons - workers, supervisory staff, management and employees and Government (state) - it creates aspect of industrial life, and may be classified into -

1. Labour-Management relations.
2. Group relations among various groups of workers.
3. Community relations between industry and society.

The major objectives of Industrial Relations are -

1. Development of healthy labour and management relations.
2. Maintenance of industrial peace and avoidance of industrial strife such as strikes, lockouts and gheraos etc.
3. Development and growth of industrial democracy.
4. To raise productivity to a higher level.
5. To establish government control and safeguard and public interest.

According to Ker Kaldy "Industrial Relations, in a country are intimately connected with the form of its political government and the objectives of an industrial organization may change from economic to political ends".

Conditions of Good Industrial Relations: A successful industrial relations program reflects the personnel viewpoint, which is influenced by three main considerations -

1. Individualized thinking.
2. Policy awareness.
3. Expected group reaction.

This view-point held at the levels of management - from top to the bottom, from the top executives and staff to the line and supervisory personnel.

Every organization should strive to introduce good industrial relations. Thus, ensuring industrial peace and avoiding labour unrest such as strikes, work-stoppages, lockouts, demonstrations, gheraos and slogan-shouting. The following are the basic functional requirements (conditions) necessary for establishing and maintaining good industrial relations –

1. The support from the top management.
2. Sound personnel policies.
3. Adequate practices should developed by professionals.
4. Detailed supervisory training.
5. Atmosphere to have active worker's participation and
6. To follow-up and evaluate the results etc.

The Role of Business Organization towards Labour Organization: From the above discussion, it is clear that an industry / business is a social organization. It consists of various persons and groups. Their relationships have an impact on the relations between employers and employees. Therefore, the business enterprise should endeavour (project) to promote healthy labour-management relationship. This can be achieved by

1. The existence of strong, well organized, democratic and responsible trade unions. These trade unions should be recognized by management. This will bring about a great sense of job security among employees which ensure that labour has a dignified role to play in society.
2. The welfare work undertaken by business organization with the help of the trade union creates and maintains good and healthy labour-management and paves the way for industrial peace.
3. The business organization with the help of the trade unions should assist machinery for the prevention and settlement of industrial disputes.

4. 'Labour is no longer an article or a commodity of commerce' which can be bought by the employer. The workers are human beings who should be treated as human beings, who should be allowed to develop and keep their self-respect, so that their urge for self-expression through close association with management is satisfied.

Thus, the business organizations role towards the employee and trade unions should be such that it brings about solutions to conflicts - conflicts between objectives and values, between the profit motive and social gain between discipline and freedom, between bargaining and co-operations. The philosophy of a business enterprise behind industrial relations in a democratic set up is to ensure the dignity and welfare of the individual workers, so that he is to develop into a good citizen.

5. FINANCIAL INSTITUTIONS

Financial Institutions and commercial banks play an important role in financing a business enterprise. Financial institutions provide long-term finance to the business whereas banks play an important role in financing short term requirements. In special cases, commercial banks provide medium-term and long term needs also.

Financial Institutions provide long-term finance to Business Organization. These institutions include the following:

1. Industrial Finance Corporation of India (IFCI)
2. Industrial Credit and Investment Corporation of India (ICICI)
3. Industrial Development Bank of India (IDBI)
4. National Development Bank of India (NDBI)

5. State Financial Corporations (SFCs)
6. Unit Trust of India (UTI)

Commercial banks meet the short term needs of industry by:

1. Granting loans, overdrafts and cash credits.
2. Discounting bills of exchange and other commercial papers.

The functions of the Financial Market: The financial market performs a crucial role in economic development of a country through saving-investment process. The purpose of the financial market is to mobilize savings effectively and allocate the same efficiently among the ultimate users of funds - the business enterprise. The high rate of capital formation is a essential condition for rapid economic development. The process of capital formation depends upon -

- Increase in Savings.
- Mobilization of Savings.
- Investment in the production of goods and service.

All these three stages are necessary for capital formation. The importance of banking and financial institutions in capital formation process arises from the fact that those who save and those who invest are generally not the same persons. The financial institutions and banks act as intermediaries to bring the savers and investors together. In other words, they do the first two processes of capital formation but it is the third stage - investment - which is the real capital formation. Thus, a business enterprise should invest the funds properly. For this every business should plan its finances, in the interest of the financial institution which lends it the funds, the society which actually provide the funds through savings and the business enterprise itself.

Financial Planning

According to Koontz and O' Donnell " planning is a managerial function involving from among alternatives, selection of the enterprise objectives, policies, procedures and programs".

According to W.H. Newman - " planning is deciding in advance what is to be done i.e., a plan is a projected course of action".

From the above definitions it is clear that Financial Plan provides a vivid picture of inflow and outflow of funds. It deals with the functions of financial system of the firm, which includes the determination of the firm's goals, policies and procedures in the financial sphere.

Importance and Need for Financial Planning

1. Financial planning eliminates waste of resources resulting from complex nature of modern business. This is achieved by providing policies and procedures which bring out a closer co-ordination between the various functional areas of business such as production and marketing.
2. Intelligent forecasting and planning prepares the enterprise to face the future. Many unprofitable ventures can be eliminated.
3. Detailed financial plan can be communicated to all managers so that we can establish integrated approach, to realize the common goals of the enterprise.

Financial policies and procedures simplify administration; assure better co-ordination with the finance and other functional departments. We can have consistent actions, better control and higher efficiency. Further, we can maintain and improve our market standing.

Essentials of a Sound Capital Plan

1. *Estimates of Financial Needs:* Promoters must have accurate estimates of financial needs. Capital plan must provide adequate fixed capital and working capital requirements.
2. *Flexibility:* A financial plan must have a element of flexibility. It must provide for contingencies. We have to also take into consideration the rising costs and provide for the same.
3. *Optimum use of Funds:* A financial plan must evolve necessary measures to secure intensive and optimum utilisation of available financial resources which will ensure maximum profitability. It should also have a proper balance between owned capital and borrowed capital, and between fixed capital and borrowed capital.
4. *Liquidity:* The capital plan of a corporation must provide necessary financial liquidity. There must be a judicious mix between profitability and liquidity. Profitability cannot be sacrificed for the sake of liquidity.
5. *Simplicity:* A good capital plan should preferably provide simple financial structure which is easy to manage.
6. *Planning Foresight:* A good capital plan should have intelligent forecasting of various contingencies. For any plan to succeed we must have planning foresight.
7. *Mode of finance:* The capital plan must determine the pattern of capital structure. The pattern of capital structure must be determined in advance. We may have a combination of share capital and loan capital in our capital structure.
8. *External Influence:* External influences like money

market conditions, business cycle, attitude of investment market, general level of interest rates, Government taxation policy etc., will have to be given due recognition while preparing the capital plan.

Working Capital Planning

Working capital planning is called upon to maintain the right cash balance so that flow of funds is maintained at a desirable speed not allowing any slow downs or stoppages. Working capital indicates circular flow of cash. It is a sort of a revolving fund starting with cash used to pay for raw materials, labour and operating expenses and when finished products are ready for sale, the cash is recovered through sale of these goods. Thus, working capital is a sort of a revolving fund starting with cash used to pay for raw materials, labour and operating expenses and when finished products are ready for sale, the cash is recovered through sale of finished products. Thus, we have a circular cash-flow from cash to inventories to receivables and back to cash.

Factors Governing Working Capital

1. *Type of Business:* The type of business will determine the amount of working capital required by the company. A banking company will require a large amount of working capital where as an industrial concern may require relatively lower working capital.

2. *Size of the Business Unit:* The greater the size of a business unit, the larger will be the working capital. The amount of working capital will depend directly upon the volume of business.

3. *Process of Manufacture:* If the process of production requires long period, larger working capital will be require, whereas, short period process of production will require lower working capital.

4. *Requirement of Labour:* Capital intensive industries will require lower working capital, while labour intensive industries will require larger working capital.

5. *Turnover of Inventories:* If the inventories are larger and their turnover is slow, we shall require larger capital. We shall require lower working capital, if the inventories are small and their turnover is quick.

6. *Terms of Purchase and Terms of Sales:* Use of trade credit and cash sales will require lower working capital while cash purchases and credit sales will require larger working capital.

7. *Cost of Raw Material:* If the raw materials required are costly, we shall need larger working capital while, cheaper raw materials will need lesser working capital.

8. *Seasonal variations:* A business requires larger working capital during busy season, whereas during the slack season a business will require lower working capital.

9. *Cash Requirements:* At time of dividend payment, taxation, interest charges, wages and salaries etc., a business has demand for larger cash.

10. *Growth and Expansion:* For a fast-growing business concern, large amount of working capital is required. A plan should therefore be formulated by a business with an eye to the future needs.

6. SUPPLIERS

An important force in the environment of a business enterprise is the suppliers who supply the enterprise with inputs like raw materials and components. The importance of reliable source of supply is indispensable for the smooth functioning of a business enterprise. It is very risky to depend on a single supplier because the problems with that supplier are bound to seriously affect the business organization.

Therefore, multiple sources of supply are often helpful. A business organization should deal with the suppliers judiciously. It should try for fair terms and conditions regarding price, quality, delivery of goods and payment. The dealings with the suppliers should be based on integrity and courtesy. The business must create healthy relations with its suppliers.

Purchase Procedure or Purchase System: The usual steps in the purchase procedure are -

1. *Purchase Requisition:* A properly signed and approved purchase requisition authorizes the purchase department to order the materials, specifies what kind is desired, how much and when as well as where it is to be delivered in the plant. The requisition form gives full particulars of stock demanded such as quality, quantity, description, stock on hand, average consumption, probable price etc.

2. *Obtaining Quotations or Bids:* The purchase manager, on the basis of requisitions, will send out enquiries to the probable suppliers asking for quotations and samples. Enquiries can be made through public notices in newspaper.

3. *Placing of Orders:* On the basis of most favourable quotations, orders will be sent to the selected suppliers. The order must be on a printed form. It must be made in four copies. The order must be duly dated and signed by a responsible person. One copy of the order is sent to the seller. Second to the production or sales department. Third to the accounts department and the last copy to be retained by the office for future reference.

4. *Follow-up of Order:* It may be necessary to follow-up the order to ensure prompt execution of order by the supplier. It expedites the dispatch of goods and assures supply of material for production in time.

5 *Comparison of Invoice and Goods received with the order:*

As soon as the invoice is received it will be carefully tallied with the order. A similar comparison will be made when the goods actually arrive. Errors and commission, if any will be rectified by the usual device of exchanging debit or credit notes.

6. *Entries in Books of Accounts:* When the receiving department makes a favourable report on the receipt of goods as per order, the purchase department will forward the invoice with necessary endorsement to the accounts department which will enter the invoice in the books of accounts or ledgers.

7. *Payments:* If cash discount is to be secured, the bill will be passed for making payment by cheque immediately. If purchases are on credit, payment orders will be issued after receiving and verifying the statements of accounts.

Types of Buying Systems

There are basically 2 types of buying systems. They are -

1. Centralized buying system and
2. Decentralized buying systems.

Centralized Buying System: centralized buying system is a system where the entire purchasing function is made the responsibility of a single person. This person is held accountable by top management for proper performance of purchasing activities.

Advantages of Centralized Purchasing

1. Almost invariably makes for more efficient ordering of materials.
2. Eliminates duplication of efforts.
3. Helps procuring uniform and consistent materials.
4. Simplifies purchasing procedure.

5. Simplifies the payment of invoices.
6. Permits a degree of specialization among buyers.
7. Ordering of larger quantities results in getting discounts.

Decentralized Buying System: Decentralization of purchasing occurs when personnel from other functional areas of a business production, marketing, etc., decide on sources of supply, negotiate with vendors directly or perform any of the other major functions of purchasing.

Advantages of Decentralized Purchasing:

1. Improved efficiency.
2. Faster procurement of materials.
3. Are more flexible.
4. Better control over purchases.

Disadvantages of Decentralized purchasing:

1. Less quantity of discounts.
2. Involves duplication of efforts.

Stages in Source Selection

1. *Searching the seller:* The search process begins with the finalization of specifications. Information about suppliers can be obtained from Trade Journals, Newspaper advertisements, Telephone Directory, routine sales calls by suppliers, trade shows etc.

2. *Selection:* The selection of suppliers start with the floating enquiry by the buyer to the possible sources. The buyer gets an opportunity in meeting the technical personnel of the vendor, and inspecting the vendor's plant to assess the technical

capabilities, efficiency, equipment, financial viability, quality control, raw material practices and general management aspects.

3. *Negotiations and Trial Orders:* Various aspects, including terms of delivery, price and quality are finalized during negotiations and then the purchase orders are released for the trial order which do not exceed more than one month's requirements.

4. *Vendor Rating:* After the trial orders are executed; it becomes necessary for the buyer to rate the vendors to enable him to determine how he should apportion his requirements among the vendors. A vendor's performance in meeting the quality, delivery and price standards set by the buyer has to be assessed in a systematic manner.

7. COMPETITORS

A firm's competitors include not only the other firms that market the same or similar products but also those who compete for the discretionary income of the consumers. Thus, competition among the different business organization should be such that the customer is helped to satisfy his desires and is better of buying the enterprises goods and services. Thus, a business organization should avoid the following -

- Exploitation of competitors by using unfair trade practices.
- Help the customers to choose the best from a variety of products which are produced by itself as well as its competitors and not prevent the retailers from stocking goods of its competitors.
- Use false claims on competitors' products which will have an adverse effect on the competition. Many a times the advertisements deliberately give only half

the truths so as to give a different impression than is the actual fact. This misrepresentation about the competitors' products should be avoided.

- Monopolistic and restrictive trade practices that have the effect of restricting competition and increasing the market imperfections to the common determinant of the consumers and the competitor should be avoided.

8. GOVERNMENT

The business enterprise should take responsibility for providing amenities in the locality where it is located. It should pay the taxes to the government regularly and honestly, so that the funds may be spent by the State for welfare activities. It should take measures to avoid bad effluent, fouling the air and condition of slum and congestion.

The business enterprise should extend full support to the Government in implementing its policies and programs relating to the solving of the national problems such as the unemployment problem, food problem, wide disparity in income levels of the different sections of the society, regional imbalance in the economic development etc. It should also help the Government in the equitable distribution of commodities which are in scarce supply, in controlling prices and inflationary trend in the country and in the implementation of various development schemes of the Government. The business enterprise should realize that it cannot function without the support of the Government. If there is any difference between itself and the Government the same should be settled by mutual exchange of ideas and suggestions and not by restoring to non-corporation with the Government.

Conclusion

From the above discussion, it is clear that the interest of

the various groups interacting with the business enterprise is not identical. They are infact conflicting. The owners want highest dividend, the financial institutions want the highest interest, the workers the highest possible wages, the Government wants the highest possible revenue and the consumers want the lowest possible price. It is therefore the duty of the business enterprise to bring about a compromise among the interests of various groups. The enterprise is an arbiter among the various groups. It should endeavour to provide a fair dividend to the shareholders, fair pay and working conditions to the workers, good quality products at reasonable prices to the customers.

QUESTIONS
(for Self-Study)

1. Explain the interaction between the business organization and the various groups in society.
2. Comment on the various sources of finance available to a business enterprise.
3. Describe the essentials of a sound capital plan?
4. What are the factors governing the requirements of working capital?
5. Describe the role of a trade union in collective bargaining.
6. Describe the various steps followed by a business enterprise in purchasing raw materials and other products necessary for the enterprise.
7. State the stages in the selection of a supplier.
8. What are the obligations of a business towards its competitors?

UNIVERSITY QUESTIONS

(15 Marks)

- Explain the various Economic Role of the Government towards its Society. (October 2003)

(5 Marks)

- Explain in brief the regulatory role of the government (October / November 2004)
- In what way stock holders influence the Business (October / November 2004)
- Explain in brief the promotional role of a government. (April 2004)
- Highlight the importance of stockholders and dealers in Business (October 2003)
- What is the role of stock holders and dealers in Business (October 2002)
- Explain in brief the economic roles of the government (April 1996)

(1 Mark)

- Promotional role of the government (April/May 2003)
- What is public relations.(April 1996)

8

CONSUMERISM

Learning Objectives

After going through this chapter, you will be conversant with:

- Definition of Consumerism
- Consumer Protection
- Consumer Rights
- Need for consumer protection
- Methods of securing consumer protection
- The Consumer Protection Act 1986
- Consumer Protection Councils
- Consumer Disputes Redressal Agencies
- Consumer Movement
- Consumerism in India

Business makes profit only when goods are consumed or services utilized by the consumer. Business is entirely dependent on the consumer not only for its very survival but also for its growth. Still the importance of the consumer to the business has yet to be realized fully. In olden days, when communities were smaller, consumer resistance was virtually unnecessary to ensure fair trade practices. Unfair trade was almost impossible in the life style of those times. With the advent of industrial revolution in Great Britain and shift in population from rural areas to urban areas, the scope for malpractice increased. Malpractice, gave rise to consumer resistance. Initially, consumer resistance took the form of comparative or selective shopping or returning the shoddy produce for exchange if the shopkeeper could be prevailed upon to agree to it.

Aware of their ignorance in buying, doubtful about the guardianship of private business, not sure of getting their money's worth, consumers unite together voluntarily. Consumerism involves the actions of individuals and organizations in response to consumers' dissatisfaction arising from exchange relationships. Consumerism is an attempt to preserve the free enterprise economy by making the market work better.

DEFINITION OF CONSUMERISM

Many authorities on the subject have given varied definition for the term "consumerism". They are:

Virginia H. Knauer has given a very simple and effective definition of consumerism. She says "consumerism may simply be expressed as 'Let the seller Beware' in comparison to the age-old caveat emptor or 'let the buyer beware'."

According to Cravens and Hills - "Consumerism is a social force within the environment designed to aid and protects the consumer by exerting legal, moral and economic pressure on business".

Peter F Drucker has given a very lengthy definition of consumerism. According to him, " consumerism means that the consumer looks upon the manufacturer as somebody who is interested but who really does not know what the consumer's realities are. He regards the manufacturer as somebody who has not made the effort to find out, who does not understand the world in which the consumer lives, and who expects the consumer to be able to make distinctions which the consumer is neither willing nor able to make".

CONSUMER PROTECTION

It is said in economics, that the act of production is not complete until the commodity is in the hands of the ultimate consumer. In a free market economy 'consumer is king'. He communicates his decision through price. He thus, rules the economy through pricing and brings about the allocation of scarce economic resources through the price mechanism. But in reality, this is not true. Consumers have not only been called upon to pay higher prices but have to settle for lower quality goods, duplicate, adulterated and spurious products etc. The consumer is the main sufferer of inflation, he pays more and earns much less in real terms. He is the one who is often cheated and fleeced and he is the one to suffer most from acute shortages of essential commodities. Thus, the need for consumer protection or consumerism has arisen primarily because of the business community has not been awake to its social responsibility.

Consumer protection is essential for a healthy economy. The need for consumer protection is necessary for the following reasons.

1. The consumer should be protected against products that are unsafe or may endanger the health and welfare of the consumer.
2. The consumer should be protected against deceptive and unfair trade practices, business malpractice and frauds.
3. The consumer must have adequate rights and means of redress against business malpractice.
4. To protect the consumer against pollution and provide him with a healthy environment free from pollution.
5. To protect consumers from restrictive trade practices and abuse of monopoly position by some business houses.

Thus, the problem facing consumers has led to consumerism or consumer protection. Consumer seeks protection, advice and information when his rights are adversely affected.

CONSUMER RIGHTS

Consumers seek to assert certain individual rights. The following are the various consumer rights.

- Right to protection of health and safety.
- Right to be informed.
- Right to choose.
- Right to be heard.
- Right to redress and
- Right to a physical environment that will enhance the quality of life.

Right to Protection of Health and Safety: The customers have a right to be protected against the marketing of goods which are hazardous to health or life. The products should not cause any physical danger to consumers or put them in difficulty due to sudden failure. There are unsafe products and unstated dangers in product performance. Misleading advertisement lead consumers to expect higher performance levels than the product can deliver. In all these respects, consumers have a right to reasonable protection.

Fortunately, the recent trend in legislation for consumer safety shows a continuous shift in emphasis from consumer-buyer responsibility to seller-trader responsibility for damages and losses arising out of unsafe and dangerous products. Thus, the shift from buyer beware to seller beware has increased the role of Government in promoting the consumer's right to safety. In many instances, responsibility for safety of finished products is directly placed on producers and distributors.

Legislation to achieve consumer protection against unsafe products is only the first step.

Right to be Informed: The right to be informed is necessary to protect against fraudulent, deceitful or grossly misleading information, advertising, labeling or other practices and to be given the facts needed to make an informed choices. Full information will enable to make informed choices. Full information will enable consumers to exercise intelligently their decision to buy before they part with their money in exchange of goods. The trader takes undue advantage of consumer ignorance and he is deceived as to quality, quantity, price, weight, size and any other factor involved in buying. Therefore, we have frequently inadequate and misleading information, deceptive advertising, deceptive packing, misleading warranties, scanty information on products, collusive pricing, deceptive credit terms, etc. Once, the right of information is legally recognized, many of the malpractice will be reduced to the minimum. Therefore, consumers demand positive obligation of full disclosure to be placed on the manufacturer and dealer so as to have adequate, accurate and up-to-date information on the quality, performance and other vital characteristics of the products. The establishment of standard weights and measures, truth in labeling and packaging, performance testing in drugs, grade labeling, informative labels, standardization and so on will help consumer to get reliable information.

Right to Choose: The right to choose is to assure the consumer that wherever possible, access to variety of products and services at competitive prices is provided. The widest possible selection of quality brand names at fair price should be offered to the customers. In fact, this should be the keystone of dealer's policy. Competition provides wide choice of goods and services. More efficient information system will enable consumers to make a satisfactory choice. The right to choose implies that monopoly is disliked by consumers. They want to buy a product of their free will and exercise their option to choose a particular brand. If the market has ample quantity and variety of products at competitive prices, buyers have an opportunity of wise selection. Thus, competition assures consumers the right to choose.

Right to be Heard: The right to be heard is to assure a customer that his interest will receive full and sympathetic consideration in the formation of Government policy and fair expeditious treatment in its administrative tribunals. Thus, the right to be heard implies the existence of a legal framework and Government intervention to safeguard consumer interest. If this right to be heard is denied to consumers, there would be no body to listen to their complaints and the very purpose of granting them various 'rights' would be defeated. Thus, the right to be heard is the most important right of a customer, as customers can register dissatisfaction and get his complaint heard.

Right to Redress: The right to redress is the right to expect every product to perform as advertised when it is used as directed. If the performance and quality is short of expectation a consumer has a right to redress. The product must be repaid, replaced or taken back by the seller.

Infact, the right to redress is the extension of the right to be heard. It is meant to set right or rectify the legitimate consumer grievances once his complaint has been heard.

The Right to a Physical Environment that will enhance the Quality of Life: The environmental problems do affect the life of consumers. The social costs of Air pollution, Water pollution, and Noise pollution are at the cost of social benefits. Industry is directly responsible for many forms of pollution. Therefore, Industry must ensure quality of community life by preventing or at least reducing the evil effects of pollution.

NEED FOR CONSUMER PROTECTION

Need for consumer protection is actually felt in an underdeveloped country like India. The reasons are:

1. A consumer wants fair trade practices. Fair trade practices will enable him to get the real value for his money and will also ensure physical safety when he consumes the product. But unfortunately, consumer has no voice in the product which is manufactured for his consumption. Hence, the need for consumer protection.
2. In an underdeveloped country like India, a majority of the population is illiterate and ignorant. Therefore the need for consumer protection is actually felt.
3. It is very difficult to effectively organize consumers in a vast country like India. Therefore, Individual consumers have no voice in the production of a product of their choice. Therefore it is necessary to protect the consumers from unscrupulous manufactures and traders.
4. To prevent the ruthless exploitation of consumers from unscrupulous business, the Government support and patronage in the form of special legislation is necessary.
5. The increasing technical complexity of consumer goods, especially those containing machinery clearly points out that consumers cannot know the ins and outs of such goods. Therefore, rational choice between and among such goods would not be possible by an average consumer. Therefore, it is necessary to protect the consumers.
6. The choice of consumers is influenced by mass advertising and other promotional devices. But the consumers find that most of the advertising and

promotion today are deceptive or misleading. He may not know whether the performance of a product will in fact meet his needs or whether the 'best buy' is really a bargain. Therefore, we need to protect consumers from misleading and deceptive advertising and promotion.

Therefore, we can conclude that consumers do need protection in the present intricate and complicated market.

Methods of Securing Consumer Protection

The different methods of securing reasonable consumer protection may be ensured through three agencies. They are-

1. The consumer organization.
2. Self regulation and business and
3. Government by having special Acts and implementing those laws strictly.

The following diagram will illustrate the methods of securing consumer protection.

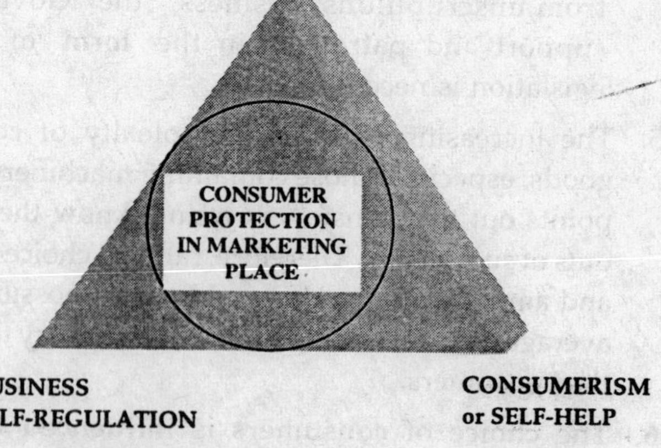

Fig 8.1. Methods of Consumer Protection.

1. *Consumer Organization or Consumerism:* Consumerism involves the actions of individuals and organizations in response to consumers' dissatisfaction arising from exchange relationships between buyers and sellers. Consumerism is an attempt to preserve the free enterprise economy by making the market work better. One of the main purposes of consumerism is the demand for adequate information on

- Quality of goods.
- Price.
- Conditions of production and sale.
- Use of goods.
- Expected performance of goods.
- Safety precautions.
- Special care and guidance regarding the use of sophisticated and costly consumer durables.

The demand for information emphasizes the fact that the consumer no longer wants to know just the source of goods and their prices. They want lower prices and quality goods worth the price they pay. To attain these ends they use two alternatives:

(a) They substitute collective action for individual action. This method of protest is used against unfair trade practices and securing redress for injustice caused to them.

(b) Consumerism takes an active part in consumer legislation designed to protect consumer interest and to eliminate unfair business practices.

2. *Business Self-Regulation:* There is no substitute for voluntary regulation. Statutory regulation is the crudest form as well as a last resort to secure a disciplined business conduct. However, enlightened and forward looking business men

are taking positive steps through the development of a comprehensive consumer-oriented marketing program. Thus, enduring and positive improvements in business practices can be brought about by businessmen themselves and these changes should be based on the inner will or desire rather than from external force.

The following guidelines may be followed by business as a method of self-regulation -

(i) *Establish a separate corporate division for consumer affairs*: The consumer affairs department should respond to all consumer enquiries and complaints. They should be given the authority to make appropriate adjustment. It should not be placed under either marketing or production department as it could dilute its effectiveness. Now-a-days, more and more companies are now creating a consumer affairs department in charge of consumer adviser directly responsible to the head of the organization. The consumer affairs department should have the following responsibilities:

(a) The company should recognize the consumers 'right to be heard' and the 'right to get redress'. Communication with consumers can be established through consumer affairs department.

(b) The consumers can indirectly participate in the policy-making decisions through the consumer affairs department.

(c) The consumer affairs department can contribute to the social objectives program of the company.

(ii) *Change Anti-Customer Business Practice*: The consumer affairs division should identify practices that are antagonistic by consumers. Visible solutions to the problems perceived by consumers as antagonistic should be developed. The various expectations of consumers are:

1. Guarantee regarding quality, price and durability.
2. Standardization and Grading.
3. Fair Price.
4. Low cost packaging.
5. Prevention of superfluous advertising and unethical sales promotion.

(iii) *Increase Budget for Consumer Affairs Division*: The consumer affairs division should have sufficient money otherwise its effectiveness will be hampered.

3. *Consumer Legislation:* Absence of voluntary business regulation leads to consumer legislation. Legislation gives statutory protection to innocent and ill-informed consumers against unfair trade practices. The consumer legislation recognizes those basic rights of consumer in the market place namely right to safety, right to be informed, right to be heard and right to get quick redress and right to enjoy civic life free of pollution. Legislation also enables the consumer's right to represent their interest in all regulating Government Agencies.

Legislation for Consumer Protection in India

The important legislations designed to protect consumers' interests are:

1. The Consumer Protection Act 1986.
2. Agricultural Produce (grading and marketing) Act 1937.
3. Essential Commodities Act 1955.
4. Weights and Measures Act 1958.
5. Prevention of Food Adulteration Act 1954.
6. The Drugs and Cosmetics Act 1940.

7. Drugs and Magic Remedies (objectionable advertisements) Act 1954.
8. Indian Standards Institution (certification Marks) Act 1952.
9. Indian Sales of Goods Act 1930.
10. Monopolies and Restrictive Trade Practices Act 1969.
11. Forward Contracts (regulation) Act 1952.

Thus, a large number of legislations have been enacted over all these years to safeguard the interest of consumers. These legislations are designed to control production, supply, distribution, price and quality of a large number of goods and services. Government has also been empowered to regulate the terms and conditions of sale, nature of trade and commerce, etc.

Conclusion

Each of the alternatives - consumerism, business self regulation and legislation - offer only a partial solution to the problems faced by the consumer. Therefore, it is necessary to have co-ordination between the three alternatives. The law helps those who help themselves. Hence, consumerism is necessary. Business self-regulation will minimize the need for Government intervention. To supplement consumerism and business self-regulation, we have legislation to restore the balance of power in exchange relationship between buyers and sellers. Therefore, we can say that through an effective co-operation among consumers, business and Government, we can get real justice to the consumers.

THE CONSUMER PROTECTION ACT 1986

The main objectives of the Consumer Protection Act 1986 is for the better protection of the interests of consumers and to establish consumer councils and other authorities for the purpose of settling consumer's disputes.

Definitions

Sec 2(b) - "complainant" means -

(i) A consumer or

(ii) Any registered voluntary consumer association or

(iii) The Central Government or any State Government, who or which makes a complaint; or

(iv) One or more consumers, where there are numerous consumers having the same interest.

Sec 2 (c) - "Complaint" means any allegation in writing made by a complainant that -

(i) An unfair trade practice or a restrictive trade practice has been adopted by any trader;

(ii) The goods bought by him or agreed to be bought by him; suffer from one or more defects;

(iii) The services hired or availed of suffer from deficiency in any respect.

(iv) a trader has charged for the goods mentioned in the complaint a price in excess of the price fixed by or under law for the time being offered for sale to the public in contravention of the provisions of any law.

Sec 2 (d) - "Consumer" means any person who -

(i) buys any goods for a consideration which has been paid or promised or partly paid and partly promised, or under any system of deferred payment and includes any user of such goods other than the person who buys such goods...... but does not include a person who obtains such goods for resale or for any commercial purpose; or

(ii) Hires or avails of any services for a consideration

which has been paid or promised or partly paid and partly promised or under any system of deferred payment and includes beneficiary of such services.

Sec 2 (e) "consumer dispute" means a dispute where the person against whom a complaint has been made, denies or disputes the allegations contained in the complaint.

Sec 2 (g) "deficiency" means any fault, imperfection, shortcoming or inadequacy in the quality, nature and manner of performance which is required to be maintained by or under any law.

Sec 2 (j) "manufacturer" means a person who -

(i) Makes or manufacturers any goods or parts thereof; or

(ii) Assembles parts made or manufactured by others and claims the end-product to be goods manufactured by himself; or

(iii) Puts or causes to be put his own mark on any goods made or manufactured by any other manufacturer and claims such goods to be goods made or manufactured by himself.

Sec 2 (o) "Service" means service of any description which is made available to potential users and includes the provision of facilities in connection with banking, financing, insurance, transport, processing, supply of electrical or other energy, board or lodging or both, housing construction, entertainment, amusement or the purveying of news or other information but does not include the rendering of any service free of charge or under a contract of personal service;

Sec 2 (q) "Trader" in relation to any goods means a person who sells or distributes any goods for sale.

Sec 2 (r) "Unfair trade practices" means a trade practice which adopts any unfair method or deceptive practice including any of the following practices, namely -

1. The practice of making any statement which -

(i) Falsely represents that the goods are of a particular standard, quality, quantity, grade, composition, type or model;

(ii) Falsely represents that the service are of a particular standard, quality or grade.

(iii) Falsely represents old goods as new goods;

(iv) Represents that the goods or services have uses or benefits which they do not have.

(v) represents that the seller or the supplier has a sponsorship or affiliation which he does not have;

(vi) Makes a false or misleading representation concerning the need for, or the usefulness of, any goods or services.

(vii) gives to the public any warranty or guarantee of performance etc that is not based on adequate or proper test.

(viii) Makes to the public a representation in the form of a warranty or guarantee or a promise to replace, maintain or repair article which is materially misleading.

(ix) Materially misleads the public concerning the price at which a product have been or are ordinarily sold.

(x) Gives false or misleading facts disparaging (i.e., captious or insulting) the goods, services or trade of another person.

2. Permits the publication of any advertisement, for the sale or supply at a bargaining price, of goods or services that are not intended to be offered for sale at the bargain price.

3. permits the offering of gifts, prizes or other items with the intention of not providing them as offered or conduct of any contest, lottery, game of chance or skill, for the purpose of promoting any business interest.

4. Permits the sale or supply of goods which do not comply with the standards prescribed by competent authority relating to performance as are necessary to prevent or reduce the risk of injury to the person using the goods.

5. permits the hoarding or destruction of goods, if such hoarding or destruction tends to raise or is intended to raise, the cost of those or other similar goods or services.

CONSUMER PROTECTION COUNCILS

The Central Government may, by notification, establish a council known as the Central Consumer Protection Council. The Central Council shall consist of the following members, namely -

(a) The Minister in charge of the consumer affairs in the Central Government as chairman and

(b) Members representing such interests as may be prescribed.

Sec 6 - The objects of the Central Consumer Protection Council shall be to protect the rights of the consumers such as -

(a) The right to be protected against the marketing of goods which are hazardous to life and property.

(b) The right to be informed about the quality, quantity, potency, purity, standard and price of goods / services as to protect them against unfair trade practices.

(c) The right to be assured access to a variety of goods / services at competitive prices.

(d) The right to be heard and to be assured that consumer's interests will receive due consideration at appropriate forums.

(e) The right to seek redressal against unfair or restrictive trade practices or unscrupulous exploitation of consumers and

(f) The right to consumer education.

Sec 7 - The State Government may establish The State Consumer Protection Council. The State Council shall consist of

(a) The Minister in charge of consumer affair's in the State Government as its chairman

(b) Members representing such interests as may be prescribed by the State Government.

Sec 8 - The objects of the State Government will be as laid down in sec 6, clauses (a) to (f) above.

CONSUMER DISPUTES REDRESSAL AGENCIES

District Forum: According to

Sec 9 (a) - a Consumer Disputes Redressal Forum known as "District Forum" established by the State Government in each district,

Sec 10 - Each District Forum shall consist of

(a) a person qualified to be a District Judge as its President

(b) two member, (one shall be woman) who shall have ability, integrity and standing and have adequate knowledge or experience of dealing with problems relating to economics, law, commerce, accountancy, industry, public affairs or administration.

Sec 11 (1) - The District Forum shall have jurisdiction to entertain complaints where the value of the goods or services and the compensation does not exceed rupees five lakhs.

Sec 12 - A complaint in relation to any goods sold or agreed to be sold may be filed with a District Forum by

(a) The consumer to whom such gods are sold

(b) Any recognized consumer association.

(c) One or more consumers on behalf of all consumers so or

(d) The Central or the State Government.

Sec 13 (1) - The District Forum, on receipt of a complaint

(a) Refer a copy of the complaint to the opposite party directing him to give his version within 30 days

(b) Where the opposite party denies or disputes the allegation, the District Forum shall proceed in the manner specified in clause (c) to (g)

(c) Where the complaint alleges a defect which cannot be determined without proper analysis or test, the District Forum shall refer the goods or sample to the appropriate laboratory.

(d) The District Forum may require the complainant to deposit to the credit of the Forum the fees, for payment to the appropriate laboratory.

(e) The District Forum shall remit the amount deposited to its credit to the appropriate laboratory to enable it to carry out the analysis or test.

(f) If any of the parties disputes the correctness of the findings of the appropriate laboratory, the District Forum shall require the opposite party or complainant to submit in writing his objections.

(g) the District Forum shall thereafter give a reasonable opportunity to the complainant and opposite party of being heard as to the correctness or otherwise of the report of the appropriate laboratory.

Sec 13 (2) - If the procedure specified in sec 13 (1) cannot be followed then -

(a) Refer a copy of such complaint to the opposite party directing him to give his version of the case within a period of thirty days.

(b) The District Forum shall proceed to settle the consumer dispute -

(i) On the basis of evidence brought to its notice by the complainant and the opposite party or

(ii) On the basis of evidence brought to its notice by the complainant where the opposite party omits or fails to represent his case.

Sec 13 (4) - The District Forum shall have the same powers as are vested in a civil court under code of civil procedure 1908.

Sec 14 (1) - If the District Forum is satisfied that the goods complained against suffer from any of the defects specified in the complained against suffer from any of the defects specified in the complaint, it shall issue an order to the opposite party directing him to do one or more of the following -

(a) To remove the defect pointed out by the appropriate laboratory.

(b) To replace the goods with new goods of similar description.

(c) To return to the complainant the price of goods.

(d) To pay such amount as compensation to the consumer.

(e) To remove the defects or deficiencies in the services in question.

(f) To discontinue the unfair or restrictive trade practices or not to repeat them.

(g) Not to offer the hazardous goods for sale.

(h) To withdraw the hazardous goods from being offered for sale

(i) To provide for adequate costs to parties.

Sec 15 - Any person aggrieved by an order made by the District Forum may prefer an appeal against such order to the State Commission within a period of thirty days from the date of the order.

State Commission

Sec 9 (b) - a Consumer Disputes Redressal Commission known as the "State Commission" established by the State Government

Sec 16 (1) - Each State Commission shall consist of -

(a) A person who is or has been a Judge of a High Court.

(b) two members (one shall be a women) who shall be persons of ability, integrity, standing and have adequate knowledge or experience with problems relating to economics, law, commerce, industry etc.

Sec 17 - the State Commission shall have jurisdiction

(a) To entertain -

(i) Complaints where the value of goods or services and compensation claimed exceed rupees five lakhs but does not exceed rupees twenty lakhs and

(ii) Appeals against the orders of any District Forum within the State.

Sec 19 - Any person aggrieved by an order made by the State Commission in exercise of its powers conferred by sec 17 (a) (i) may prefer an appeal against such order to the National Commission within a period of thirty days from the date of the order.

National Commission: Sec 9 (c) - a National Disputes Redressal commission is established by the Central Government by notification.

Sec 20 (1) - The National Commission shall consist of -

(a) A person who is or has been a Judge of the Supreme Court.

(b) Four other members (one shall be a women) who shall be persons of ability, integrity and have adequate knowledge or experience of dealing with problems relating to economics, law, commerce, accountancy, industry etc.

Sec 21 - The National Commission shall have jurisdiction-

(a) To entertain -

(i) Complaints where the value of the goods or services and compensation exceed rupees twenty lakhs and

(ii) Appeals against the orders of any State Commission.

Sec 22 - The National Commission shall in the disposal of any complaints or any proceedings before it have -

(a) The powers of a civil court as specified in sec 13 sub-sections (4), (5) and (6)

(b) The power to issue an order to the opposite party

directing him to do any one or more of the things referred to in sec 14 subsection (1) clauses (a) to (i).

Sec 23 - Any person, aggrieved by an order made by the National Commission, may prefer an appeal against such order to the Supreme Court within thirty days from the date of the order.

General Provisions

Sec 24 - Every order of a District Forum, the State Commission or the National Commission shall, if no appeal has been preferred against such order under the provisions of this Act, be final.

Sec 25 - Every order made by the District Forum, the State Commission or the National Commission may be enforced by the District Forum, the State Commission or the National Commission, as the case may be.

Sec 26 - where a complaint instituted before the District Forum, the State Commission or the National Commission, as the case may be, is found to be frivolous or vexatious, it shall, for reasons to be recorded in writing, dismiss the complaint.

Sec 27 - where a trader or a person against whom a complaint is made fails or omits to comply with any order made by the District Forum, the State Commission or the National Commission, as the case may be, such trader or person shall be punishable with imprisonment ranging from one month to three years or with fine ranging between rupees two thousand to rupees ten thousand rupees, or with both.

Sec 28 - No suit, prosecution or other legal proceedings or other legal proceedings shall be against the members of the District Forum, the State Commission or the National Commission or any officer or person acting under the direction of the District Forum, the State Commission or the National Commission for executing any order made by it or in respect of anything which is in good faith done or intended to be done by such member, officer or person under this Act or under any rule or order made there under.

CONSUMER MOVEMENT

The 'consumer movement' may be described as the organizations, activities and attitudes of consumers in their relations to the distribution of goods and services. Consumer movement involves the actions of individuals and organizations in response to consumers' dissatisfaction arising from exchange relationships. The need for consumer protection or consumerism has arisen primarily because the business community has not been awake to its social responsibilities. With their objective of profit maximization, consumers have not only been called upon to pay higher prices but also made to settle with lower quality, counterfeit (spurious), duplicate and adulterated products. Consumerism is an attempt to preserve the free enterprise economy by making the market work better.

The urge to unite must come from within. One can be protected if only one desires protection. The consumer organization becomes the spokesman of consumer. It can ventilate the common feelings of dissatisfaction with goods and services and the marketing practices involved in distribution, coupled with this, consumer guides and commodity rating or testing services form an important part of the consumer movement or consumerism. These services try to inform the consumer in such a way as to constitute a special aid in buying intelligently. Usually, a consumer organization offers the following services to consumers:

1. Consumer organization holds periodically consumer exhibition to create greater consumer consciousness regarding business malpractice such as adulteration, unfair trade practices etc.
2. The consumer organization organizes consumer resistance movements against price raise.
3. The consumer organization provides rating services which have helped to educate the consumer to buy more rationally.
4. The consumer organization is a forum for consumer's complaints, actions taken on them and provided ample consumer guidance. A complaints service can be very useful for processing of consumer grievances against sellers and securing redress from the sellers.
5. The staff members of consumer organizations write books on consumerism, consumer economics and newsletter or bulletins. It helps to maintain contact with members and keeps up their interest in the movement.
6. Besides writing books, articles etc., they also prepare and distribute materials like films etc., for the use in consumer education.
7. They fix consumer-oriented grades and standards which will offer higher satisfaction and better performance of the products from the buyer's point of view.
8. The consumer organisation lends support and actively participates in evolving and shaping legislation which are favourable to the buyer.
9. The consumer organisation helps Government in the implementation of laws protecting consumers against monopolistic and restrictive trade practices.

10. Consumer organisations test goods and give rating and advise consumers to buy their purchases on test reports in order to get maximum satisfaction.

Weakness of Consumer Movement

1. No overall view of the consumer's needs has ever been widely accepted and as a result, the philosophical basis necessary for formulating a programme of action has not developed.
2. Consumerism is a conglomeration of separate groups each with its own particular concerns. This weakens the consumer movement.
3. There is a diversity of views about the type of remedial action needed and about methods for obtaining it.
4. The consumer movement lacks a carefully planned programme of action; its choice of issues is largely the result of historical accidents. Further, consumer movement does not seem to be guided by any systematic programme of action.
5. Some of the proposals for improving the consumer's position have come from radicals who believe that the consumer's present situation is the inevitable result of an exploitative capitalistic system. These radicals call for a fundamentally reorganization of the entire economic system, but their views have won little support from the people.

CONSUMERISM IN INDIA

India is a country inhibitated by the poor. A majority of them are poor and illiterate. They buy in small quantities and are helpless victims of exploitation because of their ignorance. In spite of standardization of weights and measures, the practice of giving short weight and measures is common in retail trade. Further, most of the goods are adulterated. Again, the average consumers have no machinery for processing their complaints against sellers and getting quick redress. Under such circumstances, Indian consumers need a voluntary consumer protection and consumer guidance agency.

In 1958, a convention of the Indian Standards Institution was held which resulted in the resolution to form the Consumer Association of India (CAI). However, the CAI lacked an effective follow-up.

In December 1983, the FICCI (Federation of Indian Chambers of Commerce and Industry) sponsored 'Consumer - Business Interface' in Calcutta. The FICCI proposed to set up a permanent consultative committee. This committee is proposed to have representatives of consumers, trade, industry and journalists.

Consumer Guidance Society of India (CGSI)

The Consumer Guidance Society of India is a voluntary, non-profit, non-political organisation established in 1966. It is one of the leading consumer organisations, representing consumerism in India. It was established by nine deeply conscious and dedicated (determined) housewives with a missionary zeal (passion) and devotion. They were helped by a few social workers who were deeply concerned of the needs of the consumers. It could secure enlightened leadership from its inception and a few pioneers could attract some of the outstanding talents. Devoted men and women worked hard and within a short period of time brought up this spontaneous consumer protection society into the lime-light.

The CGSI cover 4 vital areas of consumer protection. They are:

1. Consumer Guidance.

2. Consumer Protection.
3. Consumer Education and
4. Consumer Representation.

1. Consumer Guidance: The CGSI makes consumers understand their rights and responsibilities as consumers. The rights and responsibilities of consumers are given below:

Rights

a) Right to Safety.

b) Right to be informed.

c) Right to choose.

d) Right to be heard.

e) Right to redress.

f) Right to protection.

g) Right to Consumer Education.

h) Right to receive due service and satisfaction.

Responsibility of Consumers

a) Fair deal to the traders.

b) Showing courtesy (respect) and politeness to trader.

c) Practicing honesty in dealing with trader.

d) Purchase only against cash memo.

e) Purchase only standard goods.

f) No purchase in the black market.

2. Consumer Protection: The CGSI persistently follows up complaints against shopkeepers, dealers and manufacturers. It does not differentiate between members and non-members and entertains complaints from both. The CGSI is also taking interest in preventing malpractice of giving short weights and measures etc. It also works in close collaboration with

Government Agencies to detect cases of adulteration, fraudulent use of certification marks and other malpractice. All reports and opinions given by CGSI regarding products and services are free from personal bias and are impartial, objective and dependable.

3. *Consumer Education:* Consumer information is necessary for consumers to make sound decisions while buying goods and services. This vital job is done by consumer education. The basic idea of consumer education is that any consumer law has some loopholes and not every trader will obey professional standards. Therefore, the significance of consumer education is that it can create consumer consciousness which in turn can establish consumer-centered market place. The CGSI has started a project for low-income groups called 'Consumer Education' with the help of trained social workers to give instructions through a series of talks, films and demonstration. Women's organizations are being used for consumer education and action. Mass media like Radio and TV are also employed for imparting consumer education.

4. *Consumer Representation:* Consumer has a right to be adequately represented in all regulatory government agencies which routinely establish policy in the field of consumer protection. The CGSI is represented on important national advisory bodies for consumer protection.

Consumer Protection Council

The Union Ministry of Food and Civil Supplies have constituted a Consumer Protection Council. The Council is composed of representatives of the concerned ministries, state governments, consumer organizations, co-operative bodies and Indian Standards Institute. The Council is empowered to administer schemes of financial assistance to consumer organizations for specific projects and action programs that would further the cause of the consumer.

In Karnataka, the State Government has set up the Karnataka Consumer Protection Board. The board consists of 11 members and is empowered to prosecute those who indulge in cheating consumers.

Guidelines for Business

Buskirk and Rothe have suggested the following guidelines to be followed by business in response to consumerism -

1. Establish a separate corporate division for consumer affairs.
2. Change business practices that are perceived as deceptive.
3. Educate industry members to the need for a consumerism effort throughout the channel system.
4. Incorporate the increased costs of consumerism efforts into the corporate budget.

QUESTIONS

(for Self-Study)

1. What is consumerism? What are its objectives? What is its role?
2. What is consumer protection? Explain the various rights of consumers.
3. Comment on the activities of consumer organisations in India. To what extent consumerism is rooted in our economy?
4. "Consumer's right to be heard and right of redress are the most important consumer rights" - comment.
5. Why is consumer protection necessary? How can we protect it?
6. " The shift from 'buyer beware' to 'seller beware' has increased the significance of protection of consumer rights". Explain.
7. Consumer protection in the market place can be secured through:
   (a) Business self-regulation.
   (b) Consumerism.
   (c) Consumer Legislation.

Which alternative is the best agency for consumer protection? - Discuss.

UNIVERSITY QUESTIONS

(15 Marks)

- Why is consumer protection necessary in India? Explain the various rights of consumer (October 2002)

(5 Marks)

- What is consumerism? Mention its importance to the modern society (October/ November 2004)
- Give a note on Consumer Rights (April 2004)
- Which are the remedial actions that can be ordered by the disputes redressal agencies to opposite party? (October 2002)
- Give the objectives of consumer protection act 1986 (October 1996)
- "A well developed consumerism is essential for the protection of consumer rights". How? (October 1996)
- Explain the rights of a consumer (October 1996)

(1 Mark)

- Consumer Protection Council (October 2003)
- Define consumerism (April 1996)

9

NATURAL RESOURCES AND ENVIRONMENTAL DEGRADATION

Learning Objectives

After going through this chapter, you will be conversant with:

- Definition of Natural Resources
- Guiding principles of Natural Resources Development
- Types of Natural Resources
- Importance of Natural Resources
- Policy measures for the development of natural resources
- Land Resources
- Forest Resources
- Mineral Resources
- Water Resources
- Environmental Balance and Economic Development

Resources given to us by Nature have a vital bearing on the economic life. The information about their occurrence as also their utilization enable us to analyze as to how best these could be used for the maximum benefit of the society. To achieve an expansion of human resources and capital, the existence or the absence of favourable natural resources can facilitate or retard the process of economic development. According to W. A. Lewis —"the extent of a country's resources is quite obviously a limit on the amount and type of development which it can undergo". The connection between economic development of a country and its natural resources is a debatable point. For e.g.: India is described as a rich country with abundant natural resources. On the other hand Japan has wrested economic prosperity out of unfavourable natural environment. Thus, it is not advisable to generalize and build up any relationship between natural resources and economic growth.

DEFINITION OF NATURAL RESOURCES

Natural resources can be defined by quoting an elaborate definition from the UN study on the subject. It states "A Natural resource is anything found by man in his natural environment that he may in some way utilize for his own benefit. In this broad sense, the resources provided by Nature include the rocks in which are contained mineral ores, energy sources and other useful products. They include the soils which nourish the plants, as well as plant and animal life. They include the elements of the landscape which provide sites for building, roads, railways and other structures. They include surface and underground waters which are indispensable to human, animal and plant life. Water also provides a source of energy through hydro-electric power, a means of transport, and a setting for sports and tourism. Natural resources include the air and everything that constitutes the atmosphere or reaches man by way of the atmosphere, such as the solar radiation which is essential to life". Thus, according to this definition, natural resources include land, water resources, mineral resources, and forests etc., which exist in nature. Some of these resources are known to man and he makes use of them through his knowledge and labour.

GUIDING PRINCIPLES OF NATURAL RESOURCE DEVELOPMENT

The principal objective of natural resource development is for the optimum utilization of resources. Based on this, various guiding principles have been evolved. They are:

(1) Economic use of resources to achieve minimum waste.

(2) Multi-purpose use of resources e.g.: multi-purpose river valley scheme.

(3) Location of industries with a view to reduce transport costs to a minimum.

(4) Use of energy resources in the best possible manner.

(5) Economic use of exhaustible resources.

(6) Conservation of renewable resources.

(7) Exploitation of natural resources should not result in the disturbance of ecological balance.

(8) Integrated planning in the use of natural resources.

Types of Natural Resources

Natural resources fall into two broad categories. They are:

(1) Exhaustible resources and

(2) Renewable resources.

This is one method of classification of natural resources.

Exhaustible Resources: The exhaustible resources are resources like minerals etc. The conservation and economical exploitation of exhaustible resources are necessary.

Renewable Resources: The renewable resources are resources like forests and water resources. The fuller utilization of the renewable resources is essential for accelerating the economic growth of the country.

Importance of Natural Resources

1. Initial economic activity takes place with man working upon natural resources. This is so in the case of almost all the countries. They depend largely on the availability of natural resources for their initial development.

2. Natural resources of a country influence not only economic growth, but also its economic structure for e.g.: the occurrence of water, fossil fuels etc., shape the energy pattern.

3. The more the natural resources, the better it is. This is so because the deficiency of resources is a impediment for growth. But, it should not be inferred that if a country does not have resources in ample quantities, it will have low level of economic activity because it can be got over by a number of compensatory efforts.

POLICY MEASURES FOR THE DEVELOPMENT OF NATURAL RESOURCES

To utilize natural resources, we have to keep in mind the current and future needs of the country. Natural resources have to be spread over so that the present and future generations can benefit from it. Therefore, there is a pressing need for a national policy for the use of natural resources. For this, certain necessary element should form the policy for natural resources. They are:

1. The Government must have responsibility for the development of natural resources. It is the government that can keep the social objective constantly in view. Entrusting this to the private enterprise cannot help to achieve the social purpose e.g.: excessive felling of trees.

2. It is the government that can look to the social benefit and social costs. Its vision extends on the entirety of the natural resources and much beyond the present generation.

3. The government should have plan for the use and conservation of the country's resources. This alone can ensure programming for a proper development of the resources.

4. There is an urgent need to make an efficient use of natural resources. For this, the essential thing is to minimize waste in the use of resources.

5. There is the need to take such conservation measures that sustain output over a longer period. Hence, investments in conservation and maintenance of these resources in a healthy state are amply justified in terms of the output that can be sustained for a long time to come.

6. The resources are not being efficiently used. There is wastage of resources. We therefore have to look to the alternative ways of using the same resources.

LAND RESOURCES

Natural resources include land. It is obvious that as the economy grows, our need for food and essential raw materials will multiply. Considering the probable increase in population, it is obvious that we shall need more land. We cannot over-emphasis the need for conservation and replenishment of the already over-worked soil. Thus, there is an urgent need for proper planning for evolving a national land-use pattern to meet not only the present requirements but also the growing future needs as well as the ecological needs.

Need for Integrated Land-Use Policy

The distribution of land for uses as factory, grazing and agriculture suggests that the use of these scarce resources has been far from efficient. One of the reasons for this extremely inefficient use of land is that the policy for each specific land use has been viewed in isolation. For e.g.: to boost agriculture, dams have been built that have submerged forest areas. Thus we can say that when uses of land are assessed in isolation, the claims of one use will be projected at the cost of other uses. Therefore, there is an urgent need to evolve a policy on integrated land-use.

The following table will describe the land utilization pattern in India for the year 1987-88.

Table 9.1

LAND UTILIZATION PATTERN, 1987-88

PARTICUALRS	*AREA (million hectares)*	*PERCENT*
1. Total geographical area	329	100
2. Total reporting area	305	93
3. Barren land*	41	13
4. Area under forests	67	20
5. Permanent pastures and grazing land	12	4
6. Cultivable waste land etc	19	6
7. Fallow land	30	9
8. Total cropped area	173	53

Note: * Barren land include areas such as mountains, deserts and areas occupied by buildings, roads and railways, rivers and canals etc.

Source: Centre for Monitoring Indian Economy: Basic statistics relating to the Indian Economy, August 1992.

The above table describes the land utilization pattern for the year 1987-88. The geographical area of India is 329 million hectares. Out of this, information regarding only 305 million hectares is available.

Barren Land: About 41 million hectares or 13% of the total geographical area is not available for cultivation. This area includes -

(i) Areas such as mountains, deserts and

(ii) Areas occupied by buildings, roads and railways, rivers and canals etc.

With the growing population and urbanization, this percentage will increase with the increase in areas occupied by buildings, roads etc.

Area under Forest: About 67 million hectares or 20% of the total geographical area is under forests.

Pastures and Grazing land: About 12 million hectares or 4% of the total geographical area is used as grazing lands. They include pastures, meadows and common grazing lands in villages.

Cultivable Waste Lands: About 19 million hectares or 6% of the total geographical area comes under cultivable wastelands. These are land available for cultivation but not cultivated during the previous 5 or more years. They also include land under miscellaneous tree crops and other groves for fuel etc.

Fallow Lands: About 30 million hectares or 53% of the total geographical area comes under cropped area. They include areas sown with crops and orchards.

Considering the probable increase in population and possible growth in income, it is obvious that we shall need more land for each category of uses. The various "grow more food" programs aimed at increasing the net cultivable area in the country. This was done by turning grazing lands and forest land into crop lands. Further, with urbanization land is fast disappearing under concert buildings and tar roads.

The present "grow more food" emphasis on agriculture and increased farm production without equal emphasis on forestry and grazing lands. This could be counter-productive.

Thus, the real challenge to the Government is to formulate a development strategy for an integrated land use plan with equal emphasis on the proper management of forest lands, grazing lands and crop lands.

MINERAL RESOURCES

Minerals are of great importance. They are foundations for industrialization. In fact, modern civilization can be said to be largely due to them. India has, since independence, made much use of minerals for the development of its economy.

Significance of Minerals: Minerals are important for the Indian economy for several reasons. They are -

1. Minerals help in building the productive capacity of the country,
2. They provide basic raw materials for building of economic infrastructure and for the production of capital goods.
3. Minerals have also been earners of foreign exchange through their exports.
4. Minerals also contribute significantly to the employment of labour.

Production of Minerals: Mineral output in 1989 is valued at Rs.150000 crores. The country's mining operations pertain to the extraction of nearly 60 minerals from 400 mines. It produces three fuel minerals; about a dozen metallic minerals and the rest are non-metallic types. India is self sufficient in as many as 30 types of minerals. The chief among them are -

1. *Iron Ore:* Iron ore is the 'key' mineral for the industrialization of any country. India's iron ore reserves are estimated at 2160 crore tones (i.e., 1/4th of the totals estimated reserves in the world). Orissa is the leading producer of Iron-ore in India. In the 7th plan period, the target of iron production was put at 58 million tones, of which 30 million tones were for export.

2. *Manganese Ore:* It is mainly required for the manufacture of steel. India is the 2nd largest producer of high-grade manganese ore. The annual output of manganese is about 15 lakh tones. About 80% of manganese ore mined is exported. Orissa is a leading producer of Manganese ore.

3. *Mica:* India produces 70 to 80% of the world's total output of mica. The annual production is about 8500 tonnes. Bihar is the leading producer of mica.

4. *Bauxite:* It is the main source of the "wonder metal" Aluminium. India is rich in high-grade bauxite. Bihar is the leading producer of Bauxite.

5. *Gypsum:* It is mainly used in cement and fertilizer industries. Its deposits chiefly occur in Rajasthan and Tamil Nadu.

6. *Chromate:* It is mainly used in making stainless steel. Chromate is largely exported. Karnataka, Bihar and Orissa are the principal suppliers.

India is deficient in a number of important minerals the most important being crude oil. The minerals India is deficient are:

1. *Crude oil*: Crude oil is a vital resource that the country is deficient in. India's crude oil reserves are estimated at 990 million tonnes. The country imports crude oil in large quantities, involving huge expenditure in foreign exchange.

2. *Copper*: Copper is indispensable for industrialization. India produces only small quantities of copper. 90% of the copper resources of the country are confined to the states of Bihar, Rajasthan, and Madhya Pradesh.

3. *Zinc*: India is seriously deficient in zinc. However, substantial zinc ore reserves have been located in Rajasthan and Andhra Pradesh.

4. *Lead and Tin*: India is very deficient in lead and tin. However, tin deposits have been located in Madhya Pradesh.

Efficiency and environmental protection: In exploration and utilization of mineral resources, two considerations are of paramount importance.

1. The process employed should be such that we must secure the largest output with the least cost.
2. Due attention should be given for environmental protection. We should minimize the upsetting of natural surrounding and ecological balance.

Essential features of a suitable mineral policy:

1. Detailed exploration and surveys of the important minerals should be conducted.
2. Mining operation should be made more efficient and conservation should be the most important factor of the policy.
3. Minerals which are worked largely for export should be converted into finished products as far as possible.
4. Particular attention should be paid to developing resources of strategic minerals.
5. Adequate statistics relating to the status and requirements of the mining industry should be collected and published.

FOREST RESOURCES

Forests are an important renewable resource. They have a moderating influence against floods and protect the soil against erosion. They provide raw materials to a number of industries and are therefore a great national asset. Trees are said to be nation's 'green gold'. In the words of the Planning Commission, "The forests of India are the source of many kinds of timber with varied technical properties, which subserve the requirements of the building industry, of defence and communications as well as of an expending range of industries in which wood forms the principal raw material. Forests are also the source of urban firewood and of small timber required by rural communities. They provide grazing, hay and fodder.

Apart from these direct benefits, forest perform a vital function in protecting the soil on sloping lands from accelerated erosion by water and on flat lands from desiccation and wind erosion. In the catchments of river, they serve to moderate floods and to maintain stream flow... Finally, forests are the home of our rich and varied wild life.

Inadequate forest area: In India, most of the forests are natural. They occupy an important place in the economy. In 1986-87, about 67 million hectares were forests (i.e., about 22% of the total geographical area). A recent estimate has put the forest area at 75 million hectares i.e., 23% of the tôtal geographic area. This is grossly inadequate considering needs pertaining to the amelioration of physical and climatic conditions, for the well being of the people living around these forests etc. The national policy on forests 1988 also laid down that the forest area should be at least one-third of the total geographic area of the country. Therefore, we can say that the existing forest coverage is quite unsatisfactory.

Deforestation: Though, the Existing forest coverage is quite unsatisfactory, still there is reckless felling of trees. It is estimated that the country is loosing about 1.3 million hectares of forest cover every year. Deforestation is directly responsible for greater frequency and intensity of floods, soil erosion, heavy siltation of dams, and changes in climatic conditions. The evil consequences of large-scale deforestation are as follows:

1. With expanding treeless areas, there often occur landslides during rains. This in turn silts up tanks and reservoirs shorting the life span of irrigation projects.
2. Deforestation leads to deterioration of land and water resources.
3. Continuing deforestation leads to major ecological and socio-economic crisis.
4. Wild life and plant life are adversely affected. Wild life find their natural habitat eroded, many species die.
5. Forests are source of food, fuel, fodder and manure for the people living around forest. Deforestation very badly affects them.
6. The natural environment of the country is badly effected by deforestation. This has adversely affected the entire economy.

Reasons for massive deforestation: The main reasons for massive deforestation are-

1. Massive deforestation began with the indiscriminate cutting down of trees. Villagers traditionally get more than 50% of their food, fodder and fuel requirements from forests.

2. The State's demand for revenue through the sale of timber and other forest produce is another major reason for massive deforestation.
3. The industry's demand for raw materials resulted in massive deforestation. With the cutting of trees by industry, the pace of deforestation has intensified after Independence. It is estimated that in between 1854 and 1952, the tree cover has come down from an estimated 40% to 22% of land area i.e., at an annual rate of 0.2% but after Independence, the annual rate of tree cover has doubled to 0.4% i.e., between 1952 and 1988 the tree cover has come down from 22% to 12% in just 36 years.
4. The State and the forest bureaucracy have attempted to check massive deforestation by trying to protect forests from poor people but they have done little or nothing to protect the forest from industry. In fact, they have helped industry with a wonderful opportunity to get illegal gratification through permitting illegal felling of trees.

Advantages of Forests: Forest give us several advantages, the main advantages are as follows:

1. Forests supply variety of raw materials to many forest-based industries like pulp-paper, wood-panel products, medicinal herbs, wildlife and tourism etc.
2. Forest is the source of wood for use in house construction and fuel wood.
3. Forests also provide a variety of minor products like gross fodder, tanning materials, honey, lac, dyes, essential oils etc.
4. Apart from these direct benefits, forests perform a vital function in protecting the soil on sloping lands

from accelerated erosion by water and on flat lands from desiccation and wind erosion.

5. Forests also play some part in earning foreign exchange for the country. In addition, we also derive some benefit from our wild life by attracting tourists.
6. Forests are also a source of revenue to the government in the form of royalty from the lease of forest products like bamboos, wood etc., to forest-based industries.
7. Forests have pronounced micro-climatic effects because they reduce the range of daily temperature variation, help retain a layer of cool moist air and moderate the local climate.
8. Forests also provide employment to many people.
9. Forests protect the land beneath them from erosion, reduces flooding etc., in adjacent areas.
10. Forests minimize the silting of rivers, canals and dams.
11. Trees indirectly improve soil fertility by fixing nitrogen and by adding organic matters.
12. Forests conserve soil and regulate moisture and stream flow. This in turn results in perennial flow in streams and rivers.

Development of Forests: In view of the many benefits of forests, it is essential that the development of forest are done along proper lines. Their productivity raised and they are expanded to the desired level. This can be achieved by making use of the following -

1. In view of the large needs of forests and their products, the area under them should be increased to 33% of the total land area from the present 23%. This can be achieved by stoppage of deforestation and by

increasing the area under forests by using barren lands for the purpose.

2. For the proper development of forests various facilities in respect of roads, communications, logging schemes etc need to be provided. This is with the view to expedite and expand the growth of forests.
3. Wild life need to be developed along with forests. In India, there is the urgent need for development and preservation of wild life.
4. The tribal economy revolves around forests and forest based produce. The programs of forest development have to be so conceived as to fit with socio-economic fabric of tribal culture and ethos.
5. Forests should be developed in such a way that they become a dependable source of income and employment for the people living in and around forests.
6. Another major point is to improve the productivity of forests. This can be achieved by planting quick growing species for commercial and industrial uses.
7. Forests take care of their own investment needs. Therefore forests have the quality of self-promotion.

Government Policy: Forests are an important natural resource of India. They have a moderating influence against floods and protect the soil against erosion. They provide raw materials to a number of industries. For a long time reckless destruction of Indian forests continued. It is aptly said that 'forest precede civilization and deserts succeed them'.

Objectives of Government Policy towards Forest: The chief concern of the government in the past was to increase their revenue. A more positive policy was needed. In the recent past however, the government has given a due recognition to the importance of forest development. It looks upon forest as a vital element for achieving a congenial natural environment for the economy. The right forest policy must provide for:

1. Conservation of the existing forests and prevention of their destruction.
2. The production of raw materials, both timber and other forest products, for industry.
3. The supply of forest produce to the local population bordering the forests.
4. The protection of land from erosion, floods and unfavourable climatic influences.

Forest Policy since Independence: To achieve these objectives, the government has provided for several measures and programs. These bear upon different aspects of the development of forests. In 1950, the Government stated the Grow-More Trees Campaign (VanaMahotsava). The Central Board of Forestry and The Forest Research Institute was also set up. A desert aforestation scheme in the western parts of Rajasthan was also proposed.

Forest Policy 1952: The Government of India, appreciating the necessity of developing forests declared its forest policy in 1952. It was a comprehensive national forest policy which indicated the methods by which it would be put into practice. The main objectives of the policy are given below:

1. It was decided to raise steadily the area under forests to 100 million hectares or 33% for the country as a whole. Out of the total area, 60% is to located in hilly regions and 20% in the plains.
2. The area under forests should be increased by planned aforestation. To meet the deficiency of supply of wood

in view of the growing demand, three important schemes were undertaken -

(a) Plantation of quick growing species.

(b) Plantations of economic species like teak etc.

(c) Plantations to be raised under the scheme of rehabilitation of degraded forests. Further, it was proposed to plant trees along the banks of canals, roads and railway tracks.

3. There should be a ban on any further encroachment on the forest areas, unless an equal area is newly brought under forest.

4. Forests are among the few renewable resources in nature which if properly managed, could go on yielding valuable products at an undiminising rate and for an indefinite period. One of the problems of India's forestry is low productivity, provided the forests are properly stocked with fast growing valuable species and are protected and tended in a scientific manner so as to avoid waste. In order to improve utilization of forest resources, modern tools and equipments tested in advanced countries are to be used increasingly, specially in hilly areas at high altitudes which remain unexploited.

5. If the trend to deplete the present forests without replacing them by new trees continues, we may be faced with a fuel-wood famine in the near future. Recent studies have shown that 25% of the total energy is provided by burning wood. The social forestry scheme was formulated to tackle this problem. The social forestry projects should be set up on non-forest lands, public lands and marginal lands in the vicinity of villages.

6. For encouraging industries based on forest products a

close contact was suggested between the Forest Research Institute and traders and industrialists.

7. To benefit agriculture, it was proposed to start village forest plantations in the vicinity of villages.

8. For development of forests, finance is necessary. To attract institutional finance, Forest Development Corporations is set up. The main functions of the Forest Development Corporation is to raise new plantation, exploit forest resources and market timber and minor forest produce.

9. The Central Government set up the National Wastelands Development Board (NWDB) in 1985. The objective of the NWDB is to bring 5 million hectares of wasteland per year under fuel wood and doffer plantation. This objective is very ambitious because it is more than 10 times the rate achieved during the sixth plan.

Appraisal of 1952 Forest Policy: Despite ambitious aforestation programs, deforestation has been going on at an alarming rate. The target of 100 million hectares ie., 33% of total geographic area was not reached. Thus, for a long time the forest policy in India has been a policy of tragic neglect. There has been very little element of conscious planning and development of our forest resources, so that large forest areas produce inferior types of trees. Given proper thought, Indian forests can be made to grow and supply the more valuable types of wood, raising the income derived from them.

There has been absence of vigorous policy for aforestation. Instead, the jungles are cleared to meet the requirements of the rapidly growing population. To compound the problem, there is commercial plundering, organized smuggling, overgrazing, treating forests as commercial timberlands rather than as an ecological resource, lopping and chopping of trees etc. Furthermore, the reforestation program is failing for want of centralized command, lack of pertinent data bases, inadequate scientific knowledge and research, bureaucratic battles and confusion. Thus we can conclude that the 1952 Forest Policy has failed to achieve its objectives.

New National Forest Policy 1988: It is clear form the above paragraphs that the 1952 forest policy has failed to stop the serious depletion of forest wealth over the years. Even though balanced approach to forest land-use was stressed in the 1952 forest policy, considerable emphasis was given tot the productive functions of forests, especially to meet the timber demand of industries. The objective was to maximize forest production. Although conservation objective was given importance, the production objective was given priority. Thus, it became imperative to evolve a new strategy of forest conservation. The Government of India, therefore, announced its new forest policy in December 1988.

Salient Features of New Forest Policy 1988: The important features of this policy are -

1. It has been realized that conservation objectives can be met only if bonafide requirements of the local people are met. Therefore, the new 1988 forest policy removes many anti-people statements of earlier policy and seeks to ensure that people specially tribal living within and around forest areas should be able to get their domestic requirements of fuel wood, fodder etc.
2. It has been clearly recognized that the state has failed to preserve forests from timber smugglers and contractors. Forests have been depleted owing to fuel, fodder and timber needs and transfer of land for non-forest uses and for raising revenue. The new forest policy states that diversion of forest land for non-forestry purposes will be subjected to detailed ecological scrutiny.

3. The new forest policy asserts that forest-based industries will no longer, be allowed to plunder the country's forests. The policy categorically states that forest land will not be made available for lease to industry.
4. It is a well-known fact that private contractors have ruthlessly exploited forest wealth. The new policy therefore advocates an end to the system of private contractors and replaces them by tribal co-operatives, government corporations etc.
5. The new policy makes it a cognisable offence to put forest land into non-forest uses like cultivation of tea, coffee, rubber, spices etc.
6. The new policy has made it clear that encroachments in forests will not be regularized.
7. The new policy stresses on ecological protection and conservation of natural heritage, especially the biological and genetic diversity.
8. The new policy wants to strengthen and extend the network of National Parks, Sanctuaries and Biosphere Reserves.
9. The new policy proposes to totally safeguard the tropical rain and moist forests.

Evolution of New Forest Policy 1988: the new National Forest Policy 1988 marks a significant improvement over the earlier policy. Even though the new forest policy has been hailed as a blueprint for restoring the green cover to over 33% of the country's land, it says nothing that has not been said by the forest policy of 1952. According to Vikash N Pandey, "The New National Forest Policy has not proposed anything concrete about land-laws, judiciary and panchayats to promote a socio-political-legal system in the desired direction for the development of forestry."

WATER RESOURCES

Water resources may be divided into two types -

(1) Inland water resources and

(2) Marine resources.

Inland Water Resources: Rainfall in India is uncertain and inadequate. Therefore for carrying on agriculture it is necessary to top surface water resources like canals, rivers, tanks and lakes. It is also necessary to use underground water resources in the form of wells and tube wells.

(a) *Surface Water Resources:* Water found in canals, rivers, tanks and lakes are called surface water resources. The total resources of surface water are estimated at over 168 million hectare metres per annum. Of this, about 75 million-hectare metres are available in the river basins for use for irrigation purposes. The planners' obsession with large irrigation projects has led to the neglect of tanks which at one time used to be the most common form of irrigation in many parts of the country. It is now generally realised that tanks are important for good water management and are substitutes for canal irrigation in medium rainfall areas. Thus, there is absolute necessity to utilise the different types of surface water resources judiciously.

(b) *Ground Water Resources:* About 36 million-hectare metres water seeps into the ground. Of these about 20 million-hectare meters is absorbed by the upper layer of the soil. The remaining 16 million hectare metre percolates to the lower layers of the soil. The ground water resources are used for irrigation, public water supply and for industrial uses. Ground water has assumed greater significance for a country which faces threat of draught and famines. However, ruthless exploitation of ground water can lead to the intrusion of saline water making it unfit for use.

Fisheries: Fisheries play an important role in the Indian economy. Fisheries help in augmenting food supply, earning foreign exchange and generating employment. Fishery resources of India may be divided into two categories

(i) Inland fisheries consisting of rivers and their tributaries, canals, ponds, lakes and reservoirs.

(ii) Marine fisheries consisting of the long coasts of the Arabian Sea, and the Bay of Bengal and a large number of gulf and bays.

Despite the vast fishery resources, India produces only 9% of the total supply of fish in Asia, compared to Japan which contributes about 43% and China about 18%. However, the five-year plans assigned high priority to the development of fisheries. During the fifth plan, the Government planned to introduce 200 deep sea fishing vessels to give a boost for deep sea fishing. During the sixth plan, the focus was on providing employment to the fishermen community keeping this in mind, special attention was given to family-based labour-intensive fisheries by making available, country boats, mechanised boats and deep sea trawlers.

(a) *Marine Fisheries:* India has territorial waters up to 12 miles from her coast and an exclusive economic zone of 200 miles. But in spite of high priority been given to the development of fisheries, the country has not made a claim to its exclusive economic zone. It is well known that the other countries of the region fish in India's exclusive zone. However, the country has organised coastal guards to police India's long coast and exclusive zone. This needs to be strengthened. It will take quite some time for us to protect and exploit the enormous wealth contained in our seas. Of late Government of India has shown welcome awareness of India's great and growing stakes in the sea. To exploit marine fish resources, landing and berthing facilities for fishing crafts are being provided at various major and minor ports. The programme of mechanisation of fishing crafts is being followed vigorously. An Integrated Fisheries Project has been in operation in Cochin and the major activities of the project include:

(a) Experimental fishing

(b) Production and marketing of diversified fish products;

(c) Setting up of modern aluminium canning plant and

(d) Training of personnel for fisheries industry.

There is a proposal to set up an ocean science technology agency for co-ordination and policy formulation for the study and exploration of the vast ocean potential.

(b) *Inland fisheries:* There has been a remarkable improvement in inland fisheries. During the Fifth Plan, the Central Government sponsored Fish Farmers Development Agencies (FFDA's) was started to popularise fish farming in tanks and ponds. Brackish water Fish Farmer's Development Agencies (BFAD's) was started for the development of brackish water aquaculture.

Though, there is a remarkable improvement in inland fisheries. There are some disturbing trends as well. They are-

1. Discharge of untreated effluents from the industrial units located near the rivers destroys the fish.
2. Construction of dames and barrages prevents the free migration of fish to their usual breeding grounds thus affecting the stock of fish in rivers.

Therefore fishermen have been forced to become landless

labourers in rural areas or migrate to cities in search of employment.

Government Policy on Water Resources: India is one of the wettest countries in the world. The British Government who ruled India did not evolve a clear-cut and definite policy on the utilisation of India's water resources. Since Independence, India's water policy has mainly concentrated on highly visible large dams, reservoirs and canal systems. In the formulation of its policy regarding utilisation and management of water resources, the Government did not consider the role and significance of minor water works such as ponds and tanks, small rivers and watersheds. These were ignored by the planners and policy makers. This is a serious blunder our planner and policy makers have committed. These large dams, cost hundreds of thousands of crores of rupees. They displace hundreds of thousands of people mostly poor people and tribals. They drown thousands of hectares of rich forests. But in spite of these disadvantages, our planners continue to build huge dams and multi-purpose irrigation projects and neglect ponds, tanks and small rivers.

Though India is one of the wettest countries of the world, it is not able to hold all the water it receives. Small water resources such as ponds, tanks and small rivers are misused and continuously neglected. Rivers are increasingly getting polluted by industries. Even the Ground water table has gone down dramatically and in some areas, there is serious pollution danger to groundwater due to industrial wastes. Therefore, it is necessary to make necessary corrections to India's water policy.

ENVIRONMENTAL BALANCE AND ECONOMIC DEVELOPMENT

After Independence, India launched a serious of economic plans for the rapid expansion in agriculture, industry, transport and other infrastructure, with a view to increase production and employment. But unfortunately, due to poor planning and mindless and ruthless exploitation of natural resources, we are turning India into a vast wasteland. We have degraded our soil water and air. Environmental deterioration affects human development directly as well as indirectly. The World Bank in the world development report 1992 observes that - "the protection of the environment is an essential part of development. Without environmental protection, development is undermined; without development, resources will be inadequate for needed investments, and environmental protection will fail. The coming generation presents unprecedented challenges and opportunities. Between 1990 and 2030, as the world's population will grow by 3.7 billion, food production will need to double, and industrial output and energy will probably triple worldwide and increase fivefold in developing countries. This growth brings with it the risk of appalling environmental damage. Alternatively, it could bring with it better environmental protection, cleaner air and water, and the virtual elimination of poverty. Policy choices will make the difference".

This observation by the world development report 1992 should be taken as a warning. Economic Development should have environmental protection as an essential element. Otherwise, the earth may become a ghost planet. However, the most immediate problems facing the developing countries like India is unsafe drinking water, inadequate sanitation, soil depletion, carbon dioxide emissions etc. The scope of the environmental problem is given below:

1. *Air Pollution:* According to sec 2 (a) of Air (prevention and control of pollution) Act, 1981 - "air pollution" "means any solid, liquid or gaseous substance including noise present in the atmosphere in such concentration as may be or tend to

be injurious to human beings or other living creatures or plants or property or environment."

India's uncontrolled industries and badly maintained automobiles are adding large amounts of pollutants to the atmosphere. The major atmospheric pollutants are carbon dioxide, carbon monoxide, sulphur dioxide, fly ash, suspended particles of matter etc. The harmful effects of air pollution include noxious fumes and odour, diminished visibility, injury to human health, crops and other vegetation and damage to property through dust and corrosive gasses. It also has adverse effect on weather and may result in global warming etc.

Sources of Air-Pollution: There are two major sources of air pollution. They are -

(i) *Natural air-pollution sources*: The atmosphere is polluted due to natural sources. These are beyond the control of man. Some of the main sources are -

- Wind-blown dust.
- Smoke from forest fires.
- Volcanic ash and gases.
- Gases from swamps and marshes.

The pollutants from various natural sources are minimum and do not cause much problem to living creatures, plants or human beings.

(ii) *Man-Made air pollution sources*: The atmosphere is polluted due to man's activities. These activities are within the control of man and hence could be reduced. Some of the main sources are -

- *Fuel burning* - in home oven, power plants, motor vehicles, open burning refuse etc.

- *Manufacturing processes* - smelters, cement mills, petroleum refineries, etc.
- *Agricultural activities* - spraying pesticides, field burning etc.
- *Energy activities* - nuclear reactors, atmospheric explosions, thermal generators etc.

The pollutants from man made sources are causing a lot of problems to mankind and hence should be reduced.

Effects of Air Pollution: The harmful effects of air pollution causes injury to human health, crops and vegetation are damaged and even materials are damaged through corrosion. Besides these, a study increase in the carbon dioxide content of the atmosphere is the most serious environmental problem confronting the whole world, since it holds out the threat of catastrophic climatic changes.

Legislation to prevent Air Pollution: A United Nations Conference on Human Environment was held in Stockholm in June 1972. India participated in the conference. The conference decided to take appropriate steps for the preservation of natural resources of the earth which, among other things, include the preservation of the quality of air and control of air pollution. To implement this decision, in 1981, a law to control air pollution known as "Air (prevention and control of pollution) Act" was passed. Under the provisions of this Act, the Central and State Governments have constituted Pollution Control Boards at Central and State levels and these boards are entrusted with the implementation of the Act. Whoever fails to comply with the provisions of section 21 (restrictions on use of certain industrial plants) or section 22 (persons carrying on industry who are not to allow emission of air pollutants in excess of the standards laid down); shall, in respect of each failure, be punishable with imprisonment for a term which shall not be less than one and half years but which may extend to six years and with fine, which may extend to five thousand rupees for every day during which such failure continues after the conviction for the first such failure.

2. *Soil Degradation*: Soil degradation takes place when the surface soil is washed away through excessive rains and floods. It occurs because of indiscriminate felling of trees and conversion of forests into cultivated land, uncontrolled grazing by cattle etc. The annual soil loss from erosion is tremendous and the consequences are disastrous. Heavy siltation of dams and reservoirs, reduce their capacity to hold water and thus result in floods. Soil degradation brings down agricultural productivity. The world development report estimates that loss of productive potential due to soil depletion may amount to 0.5 to 1.4 per cent of GDP annually. Water logging and sanitation are also problems in some irrigated areas.

Sources of Soil Degradation: The main sources of soil degradation are:

(i) *Soil erosion*: Soil erosion takes place when the surface soil is washed away. The annual soil loss from erosion is tremendous and the consequences are disastrous. In order to prevent soil erosion, every State Government has set up a State Land Use Board (SLUB) to promote schemes of soil conservation.

(ii) *Overgrazing*: Land degradation due to overgrazing has led to desert like conditions. Besides, depletion of vegative cover, overgrazing, is hardening the soil, preventing forest regeneration and causing soil erosion. Thus, the effects of haphazard grazing on the environment are alarming. To stop ecological destruction caused by indiscriminate grazing, experts